Photography by Jill Mead

Quadrille
PUBLISHING

New
Urban
Farmer

FROM PLOT TO PLATE:
A YEAR ON THE ALLOTMENT

Celia Brooks Brown

welcome to my urban farm...

Roughly half the population of planet Earth are city-dwellers. We flock to urban areas as it's where the money is. Money isn't everything, of course, and ironically, urban life compromises our health. We have less time, less space, less connection with nature. The concept of an idyllic rural life, inhabiting a vast acreage of virtual self-sufficiency, may be something many of us urbanites entertain as a fantasy – it is the tantalising opposite of our reality. But if we are to settle in the city, and we all have our reasons, bringing nature back into our personal urban environment can vastly improve the quality of our lives, especially through cultivating edible plants that truly nourish us.

I am a case in point. I live in London because it's the best place for me to do my work as a food writer, teacher and professional cook. I don't have time to make long journeys for meetings, cookery demos, TV appearances, and to run my gastronomic tour business several days a week. I need to stay on the cutting edge – and I love London for all its foibles and frustrations. Over the last 20 years here, I've built up a career, and through its continuing evolution, I never expected that the biggest accelerator in my work, knowledge and fulfilment would be starting an urban edible garden.

The trigger for this transformation was almost an accident, and every day I thank my lucky stars. In 2002, my husband Dan and I finally jumped on the property ladder and bought a house in North London. Whilst exploring our new stomping ground early on, we happened across a small site of allotments two blocks from home. Parts of it looked derelict, and there was a sign with a phone number on the railings, so I took it down, rang up and got us on the list. Then I forgot about it completely.

Three years later, to my total surprise, I got the call from the council, offering us a plot. We pounced on it, not knowing where to start with a 10 x 15 metre tangle of brambles and bindweed. With my passion for food, and vegetables in particular, I had known that one day I'd probably make a decent gardener, and now I can tell you: there's nothing like taking on an allotment to commit you to setting sail on the long and sometimes turbulent voyage to green-fingerhood.

Our plot, or 'lottie' as I now affectionately call it, sits opposite a church and a mosque, and a police station is within spitting distance. Contemplative weeding sessions are occasionally interrupted by a convoy of police vans screaming off to the latest incident, but mostly it's a fertile oasis of tranquility. It flanks the street, and although there's a tall fence there, somehow a barrier breaks down between me and the passing public. As in most cities, Londoners keep themselves to themselves – but when strangers see me working in the garden, so often they want to talk to me. "What's that plant?" "We grew those back where I grew up in Morocco..." "Can I buy some of your lettuce?" and so on. Random people who I might never meet otherwise are frequently giving me recipe suggestions and opening up about their past – all through the great leveller of my little urban farm. I've also met and befriended some lovely characters who share the allotment site, and you'll read more about them through the stories in this book.

I won't pretend cultivating the now abundant allotment has been a breeze. It is unquestionably time-consuming and and occasionally frustrating, guilt-provoking and back-breaking. I still consider myself a part-time urban farmer as I continue to conduct my busy professional city life but, by letting in this new aspect, I now understand the raw materials of my trade so much better. Though I'm not aiming for self-sufficiency, having my own produce has opened my eyes further to the importance of eliminating food miles, supporting sustainability and embracing the cycle of life. Growing your own is not about instant gratification – it's a journey, not a destination. It's a moveable feast that evolves year on year. I've come to realise that in the kitchen, I'm in control, whereas on the veg plot, I have to surrender to the variables that constantly throw me off track, but that experience has actually made me a better cook.

Then there's the matter of flavour. Now, finally, I realise how fresh produce is really meant to taste. No doubt part of that is the love I have put into nurturing it, and there is no subsitute for that. Here in London, I could go to a Michelin-starred restaurant any night of the week, but nothing that Gordon R. or Heston B. does to his veg will ever taste as good as mine, straight from the plot to the plate.

This book is not meant to be a comprehensive gardening manual – there are plenty of those out there and I encourage you to go and buy them. What I want to communicate is that if you have the desire to bring this transformation into your life, just begin it now, and I'll show you – basically – how, through my own humble experience.

The rewards you reap are directly proportionate to the effort you put in. So dive in and enjoy – it's a rocky road of joys and disappointments. However, the sense of achievement, the wonderful flavours on your plate, and the health boost from all your hard work in the fresh air, not to mention the increase in your fresh fruit and veg intake, will add an immeasurably serene quality to your life.

Please let me know how you get on: www.celiabrooksbrown.com

grow-your-
own basics

vegetable plot basics

economy
Any hobby can be expensive. Growing your own doesn't have to be. Sure, you can splash out on fancy ceramic containers and all manner of gardening accessories, but for the basics your investment needn't be more than potting compost for containers and some seeds. Containers themselves can be recycled vessels (see page 16). If you've got soil outdoors, invest in some nourishment for it will repay you. Healthy soil produces healthy vegetables.

tools
For containers, a pair of gardening gloves, watering can and some scissors will suffice. For gardens and allotments, the additional basics you'll need are: a garden fork, spade or shovel, hoe and hand hoe, hand fork, rake and secateurs. Many of these items can be bought cheaply second-hand.

hardening off
Young plants like tomatoes and chillies, which are started off inside, need to acclimatise to the outdoors. Once transferred to intermediate pots, they should be left outside during the day and brought back in at night for a few days before being left out. Alternatively, they can be hardened off in a coldframe for a couple of weeks, open during the day and closed at night.

where
Desire is the very first thing you need, and you've clearly got that as you are reading this book. Space is the next requirement. A plot can be any size. Plants need only light, soil and water, then with a bit of nurturing you can have your own edibles. Even if all you have is a window ledge, you can grow some herbs and even tomatoes and aubergines. I have a friend who, on his tiny London balcony, has successfully grown root veg, courgettes and runner beans. So assess your space – be it a windowsill, patio, balcony, roof terrace, garden or allotment. If it has natural light and air, you can start growing.

when
Containers are best started off in March, the beginning of the gardening year. If you have a garden or allotment, soil preparation will ideally be done in the late autumn before frosts, but you can even get these going for the first time in spring. Starting in late summer won't reward you with much, as the sowing and growing season is nearing an end. Starting in the dead of winter is pointless. Instead use these times of the year to plan ahead.

what
Grow what you love to eat. If you're not keen on beetroot, they'll be a waste of space (then again, once you taste a homegrown beetroot you may be converted). Some say don't bother with onions as they are cheap to buy, but I keep planting them. They are one of the easiest crops to grow and I get through an awful lot of onions – they are the foundation of so many recipes. However, do consider the economy of what you plant. Herbs, rocket and baby salad leaves, for example, are expensive to buy, so they're a good-value crop, especially the cut-and-come-again varieties. These are all feasible to grow in containers, even on a window ledge or indoors.

protection
The healthier the plant, the less susceptible to disease it will be, just like having a strong immune system. Pests, however, are inevitable. Slugs and snails are a constant bother. Slug pellets certainly help, but they are frowned upon because it is thought they harm other wildlife – in the city, birds in particular, though this is

largely unsubstantiated. In any case, slug pellets are a chemical poison and, though not harmful to humans, using them foils any attempt to grow food organically. 'Safe' organic slug pellets are available, but they tend to deteriorate much more quickly. There are a myriad of other natural slug deterrents including coffee grounds, beer traps, salt, and crushed eggshells. Copper wire or piping placed around plants gives slugs and snails an electric shock and should have them running for their lives, in their sluggish way.

Insect and disease infestations are a likely problem and complex subject. Arm yourself with a good illustrated manual for recognising such troubles and how to deal with them. Unfortunately, more often than not the solutions will involve chemical warfare.

composting A compost bin is an essential part of the grow-your-own process. The more you grow, the more compostable matter you amass. A plastic compost bin is cheap and doesn't take up a lot of space. Place it directly on the ground to give worms access. For collecting stuff in your kitchen, you'll also need a bucket-size plastic or ceramic container with a lid, lined with a plastic bag. As a rule of thumb, only compost vegetable scraps – no cooked food, meat, fish or dairy products. Eggshells, teabags and coffee grounds are OK. With the addition of some shredded paper, grass cuttings and a few twiggy bits, eventually it will break down through the microbial activity into nutritious organic matter – soil in fact – which is perfect for nourishing your own soil. When starting out, it can help to get a bag of compost from a friend or plot neighbour's bin, already teeming with bacteria and worms, to kick-start the process. After a while, a compost bin provides a constant supply of free nourishment.

12 easy edibles

The following crops are great easy edibles to start with, whatever your available space:

herbs – spring, summer and winter varieties
lettuces
tomatoes
strawberries
peas
beans
chillies
beetroot
radishes
squashes
spring onions
garlic

Above Strawberry blossoms under netting.

growing on an allotment

Taking on an allotment is the perfect antidote to city life. A kitchen garden is no substitute for the sense of community allotments provide. If you're a novice, it's the ideal place to start because alongside the guidance of books, magazines and seed packets, you can observe your neighbours' practices, take their advice (or not), acquire seeds, plants, recipes and exhange surplus veg. It's a lovely place to chill out too.

get cracking If you're considering signing up for an allotment, get in there as quickly as possible. I waited three and a half years for mine, and that's now considered speedy. Don't let that discourage you – you may get lucky – just call up your local authority and ask about availability in the area.

be persistent If you fail to get offered a place on a waiting list, don't give up. Seek out allotment sites, look for overgrown patches and enquire about them. Some sites might even be self-managed. Ask the

Above Late March on the plot.

Right Companion flowers including calendula, cornflowers and sweetpeas.

plot holders – if you play your cards right, someone may be willing to let you use part of their patch.

location, location
An available allotment is a rare bird. You may not have the choice of plots; rather you might have to make do with what you're given. The most important factor is location – ideally your plot will be close to home. Mine is two blocks from my house, so there's no need to get in the car. I've been known to transport wheelbarrow loads back and forth, nip over to grab a handful of chard or a couple of leeks to throw in a last-minute stew, and in the height of the growing season, its proximity allows me to do some daily watering if nothing else. If you bag a plot some distance from home, it's still a blessing, so don't turn it down. You'll just have to build allotment visits into your life in a more structured way.

With any luck, your plot will have plenty of sun, some shelter from wind and good drainage. A shed is an advantage (we all have one on our small site) and a greenhouse is an incredible bonus. Whatever hand you are dealt, adaptability is paramount.

dig for victory
The chances are the plot you acquire will not have been used for some time and be overwhelmed with weeds. Be happy! Lush weeds are a sign of good soil. Inevitably, you'll have your work cut out with the garden fork, so rope in some help. Don't try to do more than a couple of hours at a time. It may be tempting to use a rotavator to rip everything up in a jiffy, but try to resist, at least in the first year. These machines chop the weed roots up into tiny pieces, all of which have the potential to re-grow. Weeds are always a problem, but if you put the work in at the early stages by digging up as much of the root as possible and disposing of it, you'll save yourself a lot of effort later on.

The ideal time for initial digging is in the autumn – frost helps to break up clumpy soil over winter, making it more workable in spring. At this stage, you'll also need to add well-rotted compost to the

'Whatever hand you are dealt, adaptability is paramount.'

soil, made up of both organic matter for nutrition and fibrous material to improve drainage and aeration. In my first year I didn't bother enriching the soil; I thought it would be interesting to see what it had to offer as a way of understanding it better. What a silly idea that was! Soil is constantly being depleted by the elements and by what it gives to the plants; it must be replenished over and over throughout the year. What you give to the soil, it gives back to you – you can't overdo it. Our own compost made from kitchen scraps doesn't add up to enough for the whole plot, so we order in more from the council who manage the allotments.

make a plan
Once you've laboured over your soil, pour yourself a tall drink – it's time to get excited about what to grow! On an allotment, you'll most likely have more space than at home in a kitchen garden, so you can really go to town. See the advice page 10 on choosing what to grow.

Once you've decided what to grow, the next question is where to grow it. You'll need a bed for the permanent plants, which usually includes fruit bushes, rhubarb and asparagus. The rest is for crops which you must rotate every year. The three general categories are roots, brassicas (the cabbage family) and others. Most gardening books tell you to divide your space into three sections and use one for each category – alternating each year. In practice, I always grow a lot more 'others' than anything else, so my plot is a patchwork of multiple segments rotated from year to year, rather than a triptych of equal panels. For example, last year's potato patch (roots) will be this year's pumpkins (others); last year's onions (others) will be this year's kale and broccoli (brassicas), and so on. Bean and pea crops fix nitrogen in the soil, so whatever follows them benefits from this. Brassicas are a good choice of crop to follow beans as they are nitrogen hungry.

don't lose the plot
Once committed, you must use an allotment or lose it. It's possible to grow bits and pieces in a part-time manner, but if your plot appears untended, which can happen quickly once weeds take control, it may be taken back. Growing your own is a bug that bites, so you'll probably throw yourself in headlong, but you never know what life has in store. If plans change and you don't have the time or ability to carry on, you might consider offering it to fellow allotmenteers or a friend until you can return.

Each site has a few common-sense rules. Paying the rent is obvious, but even the pricier sites are refreshingly cheap – mine costs £26 per year to rent. It's a matter of respecting your neighbours and putting in the time to keep it relatively tidy.

growing in a home garden

In many ways, edible home gardeners have the best of both worlds. In the city, a garden is a premium. Converting a city garden into a kitchen garden, or part thereof, allows you to grab your home-grown food at virtually arm's length from the kitchen and affords you the space to play. You can incorporate edibles into existing borders and flower beds as well as having fun with container growing.

On my allotment, I am not massively concerned with its appearance, though when it's in its full glory I'm proud of how it looks and I love spending time relaxing there. At home, the garden is usually in constant view and should be treated like an extended living space to make the most of it. So planning an edible garden there might require a more aesthetic approach than allotment gardening, as well as diligent maintenance, so that you can live with it, admiring its beauty at all times.

A dedicated area in the form of a raised bed is a good start, especially in a small garden. This could be as simple as digging up a 1.2m x 0.6m rectangle of lawn and hammering in some planks to frame it. This is best done in the autumn, and some soil enrichment???? in the form or well-rotted organic compost should be dug into the soil. If a raised bed is plonked on top of a lawn, the grass will have to be killed with proper weed-supression techniques and soil will have to be brought in. It is even possible to build a raised bed several feet tall on top of concrete, a more expensive proposition.

With raised beds, you will have to adhere to the principles of crop rotation (see page 14), so it makes sense to have three dedicated beds. Of course, you can also have beds for permanent crops like rhubarb, asparagus, and fruit bushes and trees. You could also have the supplementary luxury of a greenhouse or coldframe.

> 'At home, the garden is usually in constant view and should be treated like an extended living space to make the most of it.'

Above Potted herbs at home mingle with the laundry.

growing in containers

When growing options are limited, containers are the way forward. Whatever the space, you'll need at least six hours of daily sunlight to succeed. You will struggle with a strictly north-facing space.

container advantages
Crop rotation is irrelevant for container growing, but for annual crops the potting compost must be replaced every year and the containers cleaned or replaced to avoid disease. There are relatively fewer pests for container growers, such as birds, city foxes and squirrels. Living in close proximity to your containers is also an advantage as your edibles are immediately accessible, and maintenance is minimal – though watering is paramount, as is weed control.

watering
Depending on how many containers you have, nothing beats a hose for the speedy delivery of water. However, a large-capacity watering can with a rose, which creates a gentle shower, is quite sufficient. Any old bottle with a cap is the economy option – just stab a few holes in the cap and shake a shower over your plants where gentle watering is required, such as for seedlings and young plants.

Opposite A potted herb garden of sage, rosemary and mint alongside carrots and scented geraniums.

recycled containers
Splashing out on ceramic pots will soon clean out the bank account. Any vessel is fair game, as long as it has drainage. I've had success with woven plastic potato bags from my greengrocer. Large tins, tubs and buckets work a treat, as long as you pierce holes in their bottoms. Ask stores and restaurants for their empty recepticles.

what to grow
With few exceptions, almost any crop will grow in containers. The most important thing is to have large-enough containers and not to let them dry out completely. The compatibility of each edible with container growing is indicated in the chart at the beginning of each month throughout this book. There are certain seeds, plants and root stocks (as for fruit trees and bushes) specifically adapted for containers, so those types are the ones to go for.

edible windowsill
If all you have is a south- or even semi-south-facing window, the inside sill is still a viable growing space. An outside window ledge affords even more space for rectangular pots that can sit securely on the ledge, providing your window opens upwards and not outwards. Inside, a sill or a table or countertop provides a surface for pots filled with summer herbs like basil, mint, chives, oregano and tarragon, or winter herbs like rosemary, thyme and sage, all ready to be snipped off and used to transform your cooking with fresh flavours. Baby lettuce leaves of all sorts plus rocket, baby chard, mustard, pak choi and others can be grown here too with little effort, taking about three weeks from sowing to eating. They are best sown successionally in pots or trays for a constant supply – look for cut-and-come-again varieties and mixed salad seed packets. In this tiny space you can also grow radishes, spring onions, and edible flowers. Tomato and even strawberry plants will thrive in the sheltered space and sunlight.

a year on the
urban farm

spring

MARCH	INDOORS OR UNDER GLASS	OUTDOORS DIRECT IN SOI
Aubergines	★	
Beetroot		★
Blackberries		★
Broad beans		★
Broccoli (calabrese)	★	★
Broccoli (sprouting)	★	
Brussels sprouts	★	★
Cabbage (summer)	★	★
Cabbage (winter)		★
Carrots	★	★
Cauliflower	★	★
Celeriac	★	
Chard	★	
Cucumbers		★
Currants	★	
Fennel		★
Garlic	★	★
Globe artichokes	★	★
Kale	★	
Leeks	★	
Lettuce/salad leaves	★	★
Onions/shallots	★	★
Parsnips	★	★
Peas	★	
Peppers and chillies	★	★
Perpetual spinach		★
Potatoes	★	★
Radishes		
Rhubarb (forced)		★
Rhubarb (outdoors)	★	
Rocket		
Salsify/scorzonera	★	★
Spinach		
Spring herbs	★	★
Spring onions	★	
Squashes/pumpkins	★	★
Strawberries		★
Summer berries	★	
Summer herbs		★
Swedes	★	
Tomatoes	★	★
Turnips		
Winter herbs		

SUITABLE FOR CONTAINERS	HARVESTING NOW	RECIPES AND OTHER INFORMATION
★		thai smoked aubergine salad, 167; *see also 124, 155*
★		*see 138*
		see 108
★		broad bean tabbouleh, 92; *see also 68, 75, 113*
★		*see 98*
★	★	psb + barley risotto, 39; *see also 35*
★	★	zesty brussels sprouts, p203; *see also 27, 42, 195*
★		lemony lentil cabbage parcels, 203; *see also 123*
★		*see 200*
★	★	*see 167, 179*
★		cauliflower + coconut soup, 182; *see also 172, 183*
★	★	celeriac gratin + ceps, 182; *see also 175*
★		sorrel + chard kuku, 36; *see also 32, 39, 57*
★		smoky gazpacho, 128; *see also 105, 167*
★		*see 108*
★		*see 140*
		broad bean + garlic purée; *see also 39, 55, 75, 100*
★	★	ultimate artichoke, 94; *see also 80, 93*
★	★	saffron rice broth + winter greens, 38; *see also 42*
★	★	*see 24, 38, 45, 57, 75*
★		broad beans + lettuce, 75; *see also 57, 63*
★	★	*see 36, 39, 75, 161*
★		parsnip, pear + stilton soup, 202; *see also 193*
★		pea + feta egg cups, 72; *see also 67*
★	★	*see 112, 131, 143, 144*
★		*see 32*
★		parmesan potato cakes, 93; *see also 57, 91*
	★	*see 64*
		rhubarb + lentil curry, 75; *see also 52, 56*
★	★	rhubarb rose eton mess, 56; *see also 52, 75*
★	★	green soup, 57; *see also 46*
★	★	*see 190*
★	★	*see 32*
★	★	sorrel + chard kuku, 36; *see also 31, 57*
★		green soup, 57; *see also 61, 72, 92, 112, 131*
★		pumpkin pasty, 169; *see also 124, 149, 162, 165, 167*
★		*see 83*
★		*see 108*
★		parmesan potato cakes, 93; *see also 28, 84*
★		hot + sour swede + cabbage salad, 200; *see also 197*
★		slow-roasted tomatoes, 131; *see also 120, 158, 166*
★	★	*see 180*
★	★	*see 150, 169, 198*

early march
the year starts here

It's hard to believe that spring is on the way, but the calendar and a few blooming snowdrops on the plot tell me it is so. The days are still painfully short, so I'm able to get the fork out only at weekends, wrapped in multiple wool layers. I do make regular quick visits to the lottie to deposit the kitchen compost and grab a clutch of kale or a leek or two, often with a torch before cooking dinner, but mostly I've just been dreaming about what's to come.

Now March has begun, so has my gardening year and it's time to celebrate by sowing the first few seeds at home. I made my first journey of the year to the garden centre for some bags of potting compost last week. This and seeds are the only expenses I should have to incur at the moment, as I get thriftier and thriftier all the time. I've been saving Chinese takeaway containers; they make the perfect seed trays, partly because they are quite small and the temptation with a large purpose-made tray is to sow too many seeds. Best of all they come free with Chinese food! Not that I eat that many takeaways (though I do love tofu in black bean sauce with my home-grown steamed chard instead of rice), but I've probably accumulated more than a dozen over the dark months of winter, with the help of the other people in the household. My stockpile of toilet rolls and egg boxes has now overtaken my shoe collection in bulk, but they'll soon be used up as biodegradable sowing pots, in lieu of pricey peat pots. Reusing trumps recycling where possible.

As usual, I was unable to resist temptation at the garden centre and bought several seed packets. As I reluctantly paid the bill, I vowed to do an inventory of seeds left over from last year and years beyond. I'm not much of a stickler for 'use by' dates, but when it comes to seeds, it really is worth heeding: they could fail to germinate if too old.

✳ leeks

Good ol' leeks have probably been gracing your plate steadfastly throughout the winter months. It will soon be time to plant some more or start them for the first time, either this week or next (see pages 31 and 83).

If you bring more leeks into the kitchen than you're ready to use right away, they'll keep well for a few days in a jug of water, like a bouquet of flowers, providing you leave their muddy roots intact. You can also wash and slice leeks to freeze in small bags, with no need to cook or blanch. They can then be popped straight out of the freezer and into the frying pan for any recipe – very handy for a breakfast omelette on a chilly March morning.

Right Cutting rocket for seed.

> **'Another lesson learned: you really must buy proper seed potatoes.'**

Seed potatoes, however, are a must-purchase every year. I acquired mine about three weeks ago, and they are chitting away happily, nestled in egg boxes in the living room, away from direct sunlight. They can go in the ground later in the month. Last year I grew just one variety called Rocket, which delivered perfect baby beauties in May and graduated into fat bakers by September. This year I'll be planting them again, along with some Desiree – red waxy ones. In my first year on the plot, I smuggled some eating potatoes from Tenerife, a fascinating ancient black variety, hoping I could chit them and grow my own crop. Unfortunately, it didn't work – they never grew bigger than bean-size. It doesn't hurt to try, but it was a big disappointment. Another lesson learned: you really must buy proper seed potatoes.

key jobs right now

sow the seeds of sun-loving plants

The first sowing of the year for me is always tomatoes. You want to aim to have the plants mature, growing vigorously and sporting baby fruits by the time high summer rolls in, so that they can ripen to sweetness in the sunbeams. The same applies to aubergines, peppers and chillies.

All of these plants have seeds roughly the same size (though some peppers are larger), so you can use the same sowing technique. Use small biodegradable containers such as peat pots, halved toilet rolls nestled together in a tray, or egg boxes. Break up any clumps in the potting compost and fill the pots or modules. Place two or three seeds in each and cover very lightly with soil – just sprinkle it on in a shallow layer. Gently firm the soil, water well, cover with a transparent lid or clingfilm and leave in a warm place out of the sun and wait. Once they've germinated, remove the plastic and place on a sunny windowsill. Keep watering with a light trickle or spray mist.

Below Sowing fennel.

Once the seedlings have their first pair of true leaves (the second pair to appear), choose the strongest plant and snip down the others so they die back. I know it seems brutal but it works!

sow herbs, lettuce and radishes These quick-growing crops should be sown repeatedly over the coming months for a constant supply, but do get a few going now – the thrilling early appearance of those first shoots is great motivation for getting this month's weekly sow-fest underway.

Start them indoors on a windowsill. Summer herbs such as dill, parsley, mint, basil and coriander can be sown directly into small or large pots. For lettuce, use seed trays or jab holes in the bottom of takeaway containers with the tip of a sharp knife. Fill with potting compost and sprinkle the tiny seeds over the surface. Cover with a very thin layer of soil, water and cover with a transparent plastic lid or cling film until they germinate. You can plant out lettuces in the ground or into larger pots once they are a few centimetres tall, or eat there and then as baby salad. Herbs can be left to flourish in the pot. Move them outside when the weather warms up.

For radishes, sow either directly in the ground or in a container. Thin out once they are about 2cm tall so the radishes have room to fatten up. Don't throw away the thinnings – wash them and add to a salad or sandwich for a peppery bite.

If you haven't got any winter herbs going yet (rosemary, thyme, sage), buy small plants now and transfer to larger pots or windowboxes, or direct in the ground to get them off to a good start, indoors or out.

also Sow summer broccoli (calabrese) for an early crop (see pages 44–45).

 late winter greens

Hardy winter brassicas such as curly kale, cavolo nero (Tuscan black cabbage) and Brussels sprouts are some of the best-value plants to grow. They last throughout the winter and keep coming back each time you cut them, unlike ordinary cabbages that are all over once you remove the head from the plant.

They are also amongst the most nutritious of all green leafy vegetables and so versatile in stir-fries, in bean or noodle soups, or simply steamed or sautéed as a side dish. If you have some Brussels sprouts which have 'blown' – that is, the leaves of the sprouts have opened up – they are still delicious to eat. All of these can also be successfully frozen for up to three months. Freeze raw, or blanch first in boiling water for one minute, then refresh in cold water, drain and freeze in bagged portions.

mid-march
the last survivors

The seed trays are warmly snuggled up at home on the windowsill; already some tiny green shoots are lifting their necks through the soil surface – what a thrill! So now it's time to survey the outdoor patch and really get some things going down on the allotment, in between spurts of rain and gusty winds. I'm relying on the old adage "March comes in like a lion and goes out like a lamb" – meaning that although the weather starts out harsh it ends up spring-like – to reassure me in the face of the more lion-like roars of the wind. As long as it's not actually precipitating and the ground isn't frozen, it's a good time to do some digging and clearing of spent crops; besides, the aerobic exercise quickly warms me up.

I haven't laid eyes on any of my allotment neighbours for weeks, which makes me think I'm a little more obsessive than the rest of them, but the sooner I get a few things sorted, the sooner I can reap the rewards. So my aim is to ruthlessly remove anything that's over and done with – parsley, parsnips, dead growth and newly emerging weeds – and enrich the soil with some more compost so it's ready for the next round. I've grown a fairly substantial curly parsley patch on the plot for the last few years, but I've decided to grow it in pots at home close to the kitchen this year. It's time for things to move on.

My brassicas are still going great guns, including purple sprouting broccoli, curly kale, cavolo nero and a pillar of rather scraggly looking Brussels sprouts. My rocket is still prolific; it too is a member of the brassica family, which explains why it has survived through winter despite a thick layer of snow in February. Nothing's quite as bold as brassicas. Chard, too, is still producing slowly, and the ever-resilient leeks and salad onions are quite happy in situ.

✳ parsley

I've fallen back in love with curly parsley. It has a sweeter flavour and a more delicate texture than its Mediterranean cousin, Italian flat leaf.

Parsley has infinite uses in the kitchen: with mint and bulghar wheat in the Lebanese classic Tabbouleh salad, in sauces such as salsa verde (pureed with basil, mint, garlic, capers and olive oil – great with fish or potatoes) and gremolata (pounded with salt, garlic and olive oil), and it can even take on star status as the main ingredient in soup, cooked with onion, garlic and potatoes.

Last year I discovered that parsley roots, creamy white and sweet smelling, are worthy of saving to cook as a vegetable. Scrubbed down and boiled, they have a concentrated parsley flavour, reminiscent of its parsnip cousin. It's popular in Europe to grow a variety called Hamburg for the root as well as leaves – a two-for-one crop.

Parsley is a biennial herb, meaning it will last two years, but it's best treated as an annual, re-sown year to year.

Above An emerging squash seedling.
Left Scarlet kale seedlings.

'The sooner
I get a few
things sorted,
the sooner I
can reap the
rewards.'

Last year we grew a huge crop of garlic; so much so
that we failed to dig it all up. This can be tricky, as
you must wait for the above-ground foliage to die
back before harvesting, so sometimes it hides from
you. Much to my delight, these hidden bulbs have
sprouted again in clusters of purple-green spines,
and we've been eating them like salad onions. I've
dubbed them 'garlic scallions', and I'd like to think
I've invented a new vegetable! I will definitely make
this mistake again, quite deliberately.

Above The essential hand fork helps lift spring onions.

sow broad beans and peas When these gorgeous fresh legumes are ready to eat, you can finally kiss winter goodbye. It's difficult to grow enough broad beans and peas, as each plant, in my experience, yields little more than a few portions each – but it's so worth it for the sweet, fresh flavour. Even if you have some over-wintering broad beans well under way already, it's now time to start an additional crop or to sow the first one. Peas can be started now and sown successively every 2–3 weeks through June for a continuous supply through the warm months, though they prefer cool conditions and won't thrive in a scorching summer.

Broad beans are best planted directly in the ground, spaced about 20cm apart in a single or double row, 3–5cm deep. They can also be sown in a 60cm-wide pot, which is big enough for about six plants. They may need support once they have grown to knee-height, but not always. The plants are highly susceptible to blackfly, so pinch out the tops when the plant starts flowering (see page 67), which also encourages pod growth. The young tops can be steamed and eaten.

Peas can be sown in the ground or in pots, 5cm apart and 4cm deep, or in seed trays for planting out once germinated. Some twigs stuck in amongst the plants will be necessary for support – their spiralling shoots reach out every which way to cling onto something. I always plant plenty of extra peas just to eat as fresh shoots in salad (see page 67).

plant the allium family If you haven't already, get a nice big patch cleared and nourished for your allium bed: it's time to plant onion, garlic and shallot sets as well as spring onion seeds in situ, and to sow leek seeds in pots for planting out in May or June. This whole family are probably the most care-free of them all and you can never have too many! Leave enough space between sets for each onion, garlic or shallot cluster to swell, and tuck them in just below the soil surface, root end down. Sow spring onion seeds and leek seeds in the ground or pots about 2cm deep. Water and weed regularly and enjoy the sight of their beautiful green spikes in the patch. Plant leeks out in to their final positions in late May or June (see page 83). Leeks generally don't thrive in containers, but you could aim to try a few in a large pot and harvest as babies. Spring onions and garlic will do fine in large pots or grow bags.

also Plant new fruit bushes (March is the latest month for this), and mulch established ones.

spring herbs

Chervil, chives and sorrel will emerge soon. Sow in summer in permanent positions or pots, or buy established plants from now into summer.

Chervil has dainty lacy leaves and a delicate liquorice flavour. Potatoes and eggs love its company.

Chives can be snipped over everything where a hint of onion flavour is desired. The tufty, purple flowers of chives are tasty too.

Sorrel has an intense lemony sharpness. Snip leaves into a salad or wherever you require a tang (see recipe on page 36).

Wild baby violets are the first of the year's edible flowers and should be popping up now.

Lovage has the intensified flavour of its cousin celery. It's worth growing for its leaves, flowers, seeds and its eye-catching beauty.

Borage produces stunning little blue flowers, but the leaves are not so pleasant to eat as they are very hairy.

All these spring herbs are perennial, meaning they come up year after year, except chervil, which is a biennial.

late march
gearing up

The lion's making his exit; now enter the lamb. There may well be more early spring tempests to come, but the days are definitely lengthening, and so is my list of chores on the plot.

As I watch the progress of my tomato seedlings, I am inspired to sow a couple of trays of purple and Genovese basil – the two are so good to eat together. I've grown rather attached to my tomatoes and lettuces already, so I will mount my anti-slug campaign when the time comes to plant them out. I'm ashamed to admit that, in the face of countless defeats, I have resorted to slug pellets in the past. My intention is to use them only as a last resort, so I'm collecting eggshells, which when crushed and sprinkled around plants irritate a slug's slimy belly.

I'm also collecting containers right, left and centre to use as both temporary and permanent pots. I'm saving food cans, large yoghurt pots and I've asked my local Turkish grocer to save woven plastic potato bags for me, which work brilliantly as large pots. I'm always looking in skips and overflowing recycling bins for plastic buckets or anything that holds a lot of soil and won't decompose over the season.

As for getting my hands dirty (though I like to keep my nails immaculate, so I wear latex gloves under my gardening gloves), these occasions are reserved for the daylight hours of dry weekends. I crack on as often as the weather allows. The process of making space and enriching the soil is ongoing. The leeks are still wonderful to eat, but I seized the opportunity to dig their patch one sunny afternoon. I dug a hole on the other side of the plot, lifted and transported the leeks to it and covered them gently with soil, reassuring them they'd end up in the cooking pot soon. They can be left happily like this for a few weeks, and will continue developing, which means they'll form a flower head soon, and this spells the end.

✳ chard

These bold greens are a winter life-saver, but can be enjoyed from year-round sowings. Several cousins in this group are differently coloured variations: Swiss chard, ruby chard, yellow chard, bright lights chard, silver beet, sea kale; also perpetual spinach – easier to grow than 'true spinach' which bolts quickly.

Eat baby chard leaves raw in salads but, once taller than your index finger, cook them.

An over-wintering crop of chard, sown in late summer, will be nearing its end now. When it bolts and flowers it's all over, as it becomes bitter and woody. Before this happens, enjoy it steamed and stir-fried, and freeze what you can. To save freezer space, lightly steam it first to reduce its size: squeeze out excess liquid and freeze in resealable bags.

Some insist on cooking the stalks of chard separately, but I chop and cook it all together – just enough to wilt the leaves and lightly steam the stalks.

Right Tomato plants in recycled tubs, hardening off in a cold frame. They should be this size, 8–10cm, in May if sown in early March and can be planted out in late May or early June.

'Don't mix varieties of sweetcorn. Stick with one type, as they wind-pollinate, and a mix will result in ill-formed kernels.'

sow sweetcorn indoors Each sweetcorn plant is a big, beautiful thing that will give you one or two cobs per plant. Considering the space they require and the fact that the yield is low, perhaps they are not the most economical choice. However, they have a classic architectural beauty that really makes the urban farm feel like a farm, and of course the flavour of the sugary juice-packed kernels straight off the plant is second to none.

It has to be said: sweetcorn can be a little tricky – I have had mixed results. Often the seeds fail to germinate, especially when planted directly in the ground – they are prone to slugs, birds and rotting if the weather is wet. So it's much better to start them off in modules or small single pots, so as not to disturb the roots when planting out, and so you can choose the healthiest specimens. They need a long, warm growing season, so get them started indoors or in a greenhouse now or up until late April. From May they can be sown directly outdoors, but you may be disappointed with the results. Don't mix varieties of sweetcorn. Stick with one type, as they wind-pollinate, and a mix will result in ill-formed kernels.

The seeds can be chitted – germinated before planting, in the dark between two damp paper towel layers – so that you can choose the ones that are guaranteed runners. You'll need at least 10–12 plants for successful pollination so, if growing in containers, plan for several large pots each holding 3–4 plants.

Plant the dry seeds or chitted seeds about 2cm deep in small pots. Once they've grown to about 10cm tall, each seedling should be planted out in a block, not a row, about 45cm apart. Planting in a block encourages successful pollination by the wind.

sow globe artichokes

If you have some space in the ground or a giant container, you simply must grow some artichokes. I grew mine from seed in my first year on the allotment, and I now have the most beautiful giant plants which produce dozens of my favourite vegetable all through the summer. These remarkable plants are actually giant thistles, and I always let a few of them go past the eating stage and burst into gorgeous purple flowers.

Grow artichokes from seed sprinkled lightly in a tray of compost, from bought seedlings, or from suckers off one of your neighbours' plants. They'll need a permanent position, though, so choose wisely. That said, you can always dig them up in future if you find them overwhelming.

sow celeriac

Celeriac is a bulbous root vegetable, though a good deal of the actual roots are spindly underground strings that have to be cut away before eating. It is a sister to celery, parsnip and parsley, and the leaves of all those plants look similar. I've never been able to grow very plump specimens and always have to cut off loads of rootage, but the homegrown taste is phenomenal of course!

Celeriac is a slow developer, but is easy to grow from seed indoors in a tray, to be planted out in the ground or a huge tub once several flat parsley-like leaves have formed. Never let the plants dry out – they like it moist.

also

Common fennel (the herb) and Florence fennel (the vegetable) can be sown in a tray or pot in the greenhouse or on the windowsill from now through June (see page 140).

purple sprouting broccoli

Affectionately referred to as PSB, this wonderful plant rules the patch as winter wanes. All winter long, it graces the plot-scape with its beautiful dew catching blue-green foliage; then, as soon as the season hints at changing, it throws out its purple flower buds. You must catch them before they burst into yellow flowers, and you can eat them stem and all, as well as the tender leaves. The more you cut, the more the sprouts insist on coming back. If you can't keep up with the crop, simply trim, wash, blanch, and freeze in bags.

PSB ticks all the boxes: there's a variety for every time of year, it's easy to grow (if you have space), prolific, money-saving, a natural life-extending superfood, and thoroughly delicious. Steamed, stir-fried or roasted, PSB pairs well with Asian flavours like soy, chilli, lime and sesame. It loves the company of eggs and cheese. Stir-fry some chopped stalks with garlic, spring onions and chilli and stir into cooked pasta with a squeeze of lemon and top with Parmesan.

sorrel + chard kuku

A kuku is a Persian-style omelette: a solid, torte-like affair with any manner of veg and a few nuts and dried fruits thrown in, served cut into wedges. Sorrel gives this a tangy edge, but you could use any greens to make up the 300g weight. You'll find bright red dried barberries in Middle Eastern food shops. Eat this at any temperature, but cold is definitely best.

2 tbsp barberries or sultanas
1 tbsp virgin rapeseed oil or olive oil plus 2 tsp
2 medium onions, chopped
200g chard leaves with stems, chopped
100g sorrel leaves, stems removed, chopped
50g pine nuts
6 organic eggs
4 tbsp cottage cheese
Sea salt and freshly ground black pepper
Pinch of cayenne pepper
Handful of fresh parsley, chopped

Preheat the grill to high, or preheat the oven to 200°C (400°F).

Place the sultanas in a bowl and pour boiling water over them. Leave to soak while you prepare the rest of the kuku.

Heat a medium non-stick, oven-safe frying pan over a moderate heat and add 1 tbsp oil. Add the onions and cook until golden. Remove to a large bowl.

Add the chopped greens to the pan with a pinch of salt and cook, stirring, until wilted. Drain in a colander. Add the wilted greens to the bowl with the onions. Drain the sultanas and add to the bowl, along with the pine nuts, and mix together. Push the bowl contents to one side and add the eggs, cottage cheese, salt, pepper and cayenne. Beat these together until evenly combined, then incorporate the greens mixture.

Heat the pan again over a low heat and add the 2 tsp oil. Pour in the egg mixture and smooth the top. Keep loosening the edge of the kuku with a spatula. Cook for about 10–15 minutes until golden underneath and slightly withdrawn from the edges. Place the pan under the grill or in the oven and cook until golden and set on top, about 5 minutes.

Cool briefly, then shake the pan to loosen. Turn out the kuku onto a large plate. Leave to cool, then chill. Serve in wedges with chopped parsley. **Serves 4–6**

Prep tip Weigh the trimmed greens before washing them.

saffron rice broth with late winter greens

Kale, cavolo nero (Tuscan black cabbage), Brussels sprouts, or just about any dark green winter leaves can be used in this comforting winter broth, intensely flavoured with saffron and porcini mushrooms. Brown rice makes this dish particularly healthy, but you could use any rice – risotto rice would be best.

2 tbsp olive oil, plus more
   to finish
2 leeks, trimmed and finely
   sliced
150g short grain brown rice
1.5 litres well-flavoured stock
20g dried porcini mushrooms,
   rinsed
2 large pinches of saffron,
   about 100 strands
4 large handfuls of winter
   greens (about 120g
   prepared weight), cleaned
   and roughly chopped
Freshly ground black pepper
Freshly grated Parmesan,
   to finish

Heat a large saucepan over a medium heat and add the oil. Fry the leeks until soft and lightly golden. Add the rice and stir to coat, then add the stock with the mushrooms and saffron. Bring to the boil and then simmer, stirring occasionally, until the rice is cooked.

Add the greens and cook until tender, about 5–7 minutes. Ladle into bowls, add a few drops of olive oil, grind over some pepper and shower with freshly grated Parmesan.
Serves 4

Prep tip Save the leek greens after trimming. Wash them thoroughly, then boil in water with a little salt to make a stock. If using kale or cavolo nero, use a brush to clean the underside of the leaves under cold running water, then tear the tender leaves away from the tough stalks.

psb + barley risotto

Pearl barley's wonderfully chewy, chunky grains are a wholesome substitute for risotto rice and a good vehicle for purple sprouting broccoli. Use this recipe as a foundation for other seasonal veg as well – peas, broad beans, asparagus, sweetcorn, and fennel would all work well in place of the broccoli.

2 tbsp olive oil
1 large onion, chopped
3 cloves garlic, chopped
250g pearl barley
250ml white wine or vermouth
1 litre well-flavoured stock
Finely grated zest of 1 lemon
Sea salt and freshly ground
   black pepper

150g purple sprouting
   broccoli, full florets,
   stems chopped
2 tbsp freshly grated
   Parmesan, plus more
   to finish

Heat a large pan over a low to medium heat and add the oil. Add onion and sauté until soft and translucent. Add the garlic and pearl barley, stir until the garlic is fragrant, then pour in the wine. Simmer until the wine is completely absorbed, then add the stock and lemon zest and season with salt and pepper. Cook, stirring occasionally, until the barley is tender and the liquid is nearly absorbed but still a little soupy, about 35–45 minutes. (Unlike risotto rice, barley isn't 'ruined' by overcooking and allows for less precision in determining when it's done – though it is nice if it's served slightly al dente.)

Five minutes before serving, add the purple sprouting broccoli, stir and cover. Cook until the PSB is bright green and lightly cooked. Stir through 2 tbsp Parmesan. Serve in warm bowls with plenty more Parmesan. **Serves 4**

Prep tip Soak the PSB in cold water with a dash of vinegar added for a few minutes to ensure any hidden insects make a swift exit.

smoky chard with chickpeas

A quick supper – serve as is or with couscous or rice.

Drain the contents of a tin of chickpeas, then stir-fry with chopped garlic in olive oil. Add a few handfuls of shredded chard with a little salt and pepper and stir until wilted. Stir in some pimentón (smoked paprika), then add a squeeze of lemon juice.

Serve topped with yoghurt flavoured with lemon, salt and ground cumin.

APRIL	INDOORS OR UNDER GLASS	OUTDOORS DIRECT IN SOIL
Asparagus		★
Aubergines	★	
Beetroot		★
Brassica shoots and leaves		
Broad beans		★
Broccoli (calabrese)	★	
Broccoli (sprouting)	★	★
Brussel sprouts	★	★
Cabbage (spring)		
Cabbage (summer/winter)	★	★
Carrots		★
Cauliflower	★	★
Celeriac	★	★
Chard	★	★
Courgettes	★	
Cucumbers	★	
Fennel	★	
Flowers (edible/companion)	★	★
Garlic		★
Globe artichokes		★
Kale	★	★
Leeks	★	★
Lettuce/salad leaves	★	★
Nettles		
Onions/shallots		★
Parnsips		★
Peas	★	★
Peppers and chillies	★	
Perpetual spinach	★	★
Potatoes		★
Radishes	★	★
Rhubarb		★
Rocket	★	★
Runner beans/other beans	★	★
Salsify/scorzonera		★
Spinach	★	★
Spring herbs	★	★
Spring onions	★	★
Squashes/pumpkins	★	
Strawberries	★	★
Summer herbs	★	★
Swedes		★
Sweetcorn	★	
Tomatoes	★	
Turnips		★
Winter herbs	★	★

UITABLE FOR CONTAINERS	HARVESTING NOW	RECIPES AND OTHER INFORMATION
★	★	asparagus, lentil + ricotta parcels, 55; *see also* 50
★		thai smoked aubergine salad, 167; *see also* 124, 155
★		*see* 138
	★	*see* 27
★		broad bean tabbouleh, 92; *see also* 68, 75, 112
★		*see* 98
★	★	psb + barley risotto, 39; *see also* 35
★		zesty brussels sprouts, 203; *see also* 27, 42, 195
★	★	lemony lentil cabbage parcels, 203; *see also* 123
★		*see* 123, 200, 203
★		*see* 167, 179
★	★	cauliflower + coconut soup, 182; *see also* 172, 183
★		celeriac gratin + ceps, 182, *see also* 175
★	★	sorrel + chard kuku, 36; *see also* 32, 39, 57
★		warm courgette salad, 113; *see also* 102, 128, 148
★		smoky gazpacho, 128; *see also* 105, 167
★		*see* 140
★		*see* 116
★		broad bean + garlic purée; *see* 39, 55, 75, 100
		ultimate artichoke, 94; *see also* 80, 93
★	★	saffron rice broth + winter greens, 38; *see also* 42
★	★	*see* 24, 38, 45, 57, 75
★	★	broad beans + lettuce, 75; *see also* 57, 63
	★	green soup, 57; *see also* 48
★		*see* 36, 39, 75, 161
★		parsnip, pear + stilton soup, 202; *see also* 193
★		pea + feta egg cups, 72; *see also* 67
★		*see* 112, 131, 143, 144
★	★	*see* 32
★		parmesan potato cakes, 93; *see also* 57, 91
★	★	*see* 64
	★	rhubarb + lentil curry, 75; *see also* 52, 56
★	★	green soup, 57; *see also* 46
★		soy glazed runner beans, 112; *see also* 106, 127, 131
★		*see* 190
★	★	*see* 32
★	★	sorrel + chard kuku, 36; *see also* 31, 57
★	★	green soup, 57; *see also* 61, 72, 92, 112, 131
★		pumpkin pasty, 169; *see also* 124, 149, 162, 165, 167
★		*see* 83
★		parmesan potato cakes, 93; *see also* 28, 84
★		hot + sour swede + cabbage salad, 200; *see also* 197
★		sweetcorn + spiced avocado soup, 131; *see also* 119
★		slow-roasted tomatoes, 131; *see also* 120, 158, 166
★		*see* 180
★	★	*see* 150, 169, 198

early april
two shed fred

Fred looks after two plots in our eight-plot site. He's retired, so he's got a little extra time on his hands. He goes back home to Jamaica for the winter, but now he's back and hard at work. A lady called Miss Gaynor, also from Jamaica, lives in the house adjacent to the site. She's got a plot next to Fred's, and he manages to cultivate a portion of her plot as well. Last week she was out there digging away, with her Manx cat Patch rubbing at her feet. I asked when Fred was returning. "He'll be back soon," she said, "and when Fred come back, he put us all to shame."

Too right. Other than sheer elbow grease, I don't know how he does it. His crops are always bigger and better than everyone else's, and his huge space is always immaculate and weed-free. And he doesn't lift a finger, let alone a fork, over the winter months, as he's on the other side of the planet! I can see I'm set for another season of green envy.

Fred is a mine of knowledge and a great advisor on the plot, naturally. Since the beginning, he's been very supportive of our progress and gently nudged us when we were clueless. In the first year he showed us how to earth up our potatoes, and has always been a generous donator of seeds and baby plants (his Caribbean pumpkin is one of the best ever, and I've regenerated the seeds over and over again). I'll never forget him observing my first-ever carrot rows and saying, "You've got some good strong carrots there." "Thanks!" I said, beaming with pride. "But you know, you must thin them out some more. If you don't thin them out, they don't have room to grow."

This lesson has stuck with me, and I've become hardened to the murderous process of thinning out perfectly good seedlings. Luckily I've also learned that in most cases you can eat the thinnings, and very tasty they are too!

✳ brassica shoots and leaves

I discovered quite by accident that PSB isn't the only sprouting wonder vegetable. You can get extra mileage out of your curly kale, Brussels sprouts and cavolo nero too if you let them stick around into early spring.

Just like all their cabbagey cousins, they'll want to reproduce when spring is in the air, and throw out flowering shoots. While the shoots are still budding, before they open, cut them and treat just as you would PSB, and use the new leaves as well. Sweet and tender, they are wonderful just steamed or lightly stir-fried.

Right Harvesting mixed leaves for green soup (see recipe on page 57).

'There's always something going on, brassica-wise, from glut to germination to growth.'

sow brassicas As last year's crops come to an end, it's time to get this year's going. There's always something going on, brassica-wise, from glut to germination to growth. These stupendous plants take a lot of space, a lot of time, and a lot out of the soil, but they give it all back to you in the form of satisfaction and nutrition. Swedes, turnips, radishes and rocket are also brassicas, but they are covered elsewhere in this book (see pages 46, 64, 67 104, 180 and 197).

I mostly grow brassicas that are cut-and-come-again like kale, cavolo nero and purple sprouting broccoli, plus some summer broccoli or calabrese. I grow four or five of each, with a few extra on the broccoli front as it's my favourite. Most cabbages and cauliflowers are wonderful to grow, but after the long time they take to develop, you cut them and it's all over for the entire plant. Most brassicas will take up to a metre square to grow, and are often even taller than that, but you can still grow them in heavy containers so they don't topple in the wind. Look for varieties specially suited for containers. Summer cabbages take up less space.

You can start your seeds off now in small pots or trays. (You can still get some summer broccoli going now, but it's best to sow it in March to be ready midsummer.) Brassica seeds are miniscule round balls, variations on their mustard-seed cousins. Take a few pinches of seed and scatter in 10–15cm pots and cover lightly with soil. When the seedlings are about 10–13cm high, plant out the strongest into their final positions, once you determine how many plants you have space for. Birds, especially pigeons, will make mincemeat out of them if you don't protect them with some basic netting. Even rows of thread stretched between sticks above the plants act as a deterrent. CDs or little mirrors dangling from strings also help.

Below Scarlet kale.

plant potatoes

Easter is the traditional time for planting out your chitted (pre-sprouted) seed potatoes into the ground or in containers. In fact, potatoes grow successfully in thick plastic potting compost bags. Remove about three-quarters of the compost, roll down the plastic, puncture a few holes in the bag and put three seed potatoes in. Just cover with compost. Keep moist and, as the green growth peeks out, keep covering with more soil, gradually unrolling the bag. Eventually the bag will be nearly full again and you can leave the plants to grow above the surface. By midsummer, the plants will flower, which means the potatoes should be ready – have a poke around to see if they are big enough. Then just cut open the bag to harvest. There are also specially designed potato barrels, or any large, wide cylindrical container with good drainage will do. Good compost is a must.

The same applies in the vegetable garden or plot. Plant seed potatoes, with the shoots facing upwards, in trenches about 13cm deep and 30cm apart, and as the foliage shows they should be 'earthed up' continuously by covering with soil, encouraging strong, healthy plants.

I usually grow two types a year: one set of earlies and one maincrop, but only enough to eat fresh. I don't see the point in growing enough to store over the winter months. In my urban farm, I don't have to aim for complete self-sufficiency. They taste best fresh out of the ground, I don't have space to store them, and during the off-season they are cheap enough to buy.

also April is the month to plant asparagus crowns for the first time. It will need a well-nourished permanent position where you can dig a trench 30cm wide and 20cm deep, burying the crowns with 5cm of soil. It can be productive for up to twenty years. Asparagus is not recommended to be grown in containers, but it could be attempted in a very large tub for a small annual harvest.

late-season leeks

If you haven't finished off your leeks by now, this could be the end. If any have started to form a flower head, they need to be dug up immediately.

Most likely, when you cut into them, they will show a thickening translucent core. They may still be tender enough to eat – try briefly boiling a small piece and taste it. If it is not too tough to eat, cook as normal. If it is tough, you can still slice them up and boil them in salted water to cover for about 15 minutes, mash with a potato masher, then strain the potent leeky stock and use for soup or risotto, or freeze.

mid-april
asparagus, alex and animals

It's a thrill a minute down at the plot, as things wake up from their winter slumber. The first purple-pink asparagus heads make their annual debut and grace our plates daily, freshly cut and steamed as soon as I can get them home for maximum sweetness. The rhubarb seems to be on steroids, throwing out more stalks and humongous leaves than I can possibly cope with: I'm cooking it, processing it, or giving it away to all and sundry. Offering it to my plot neighbours is a bit like carrying coals to Newcastle (they've all got ample rhubarb), but plenty of friends and passers-by take a load off me. Despite it being the height of the rhubarb season, it's ridiculously expensive to buy in the supermarket.

The sun is coming out to play more regularly and my plot-pals and a variety of frisky animals are out in force as well. Alex from Plot 6 is rarely seen (he's recently become a dad), but when he does make it down, he goes hell for leather. I watch in awe and envy as, in less than an hour, he installs a perfectly formed raised bed and plants several healthy shoots of peas, mangetout and dwarf beans over half the new bed. On the other half, he lays down wire mesh as an anti-cat defence. As soon as he packs up and leaves, the cat I call Sandy Puss trots over it obliviously on some kind of mission. Next thing I know, Sandy Puss and Slinky Puss confront the local city fox. They corner him in Alex's greenhouse, but he finds a hole and escapes. I hope they scared the living daylights out of him: I recognise his paw prints in my onion patch, the scoundrel.

Tending my urban farm has turned me into a keen forager, and this time of year sees the first of the loot from the wild. It's too early to find much in the city's green spaces apart from young nettles, but I don't have to travel far to find some choice food for free. Ramsons, or wild garlic leaves, are

✳ rocket

Rocket has to be the plot's best-value crop. It's so quick and simple to grow, and once cut it just keeps coming. Even when it bolts and sports delicate white blossoms with chocolate-coloured streaks, the leaves are still deliciously peppery, if a little coarser than before. (It might not come to this in a small window box, but will do if growing in the ground or a large pot.)

I keep a rocket patch going all winter, but now it's time for more to be sown every few weeks until autumn.

At the leggy stage, the leaves are large, prolific and perfect for soup. The flowers themselves are a real treat. They have a sweet-savoury flavour oddly reminiscent of bacon. I constantly nibble rocket flowers each time I pass the patch, as well as bring them home to sprinkle over salads or just about anything. Cut stems of blooming rocket keep well in a vase of water.

Right Pick rhubarb by pulling from the base, rather than cutting.

 nettles

I've always considered stinging nettles more of a foe than a friend – how could something that can inflict hours of itchy pain just from a second's contact with the skin possibly be edible? Not only that, but as a highly successful botanical species, they are a right royal pain all over the plot in weed form. But wait! It's true – as soon as they meet the heat of the cooking pan, they are converted from enemy to a tasty green vegetable with herbal notes in the flavour.

Making nettle soup is another of my 'hello spring' rituals, and they are equally good as a side vegetable, sautéed in olive oil with garlic. Just be sure to wear thick gloves when picking and toss them into a bag. It's the younger specimens or the tops of maturing spring nettles that taste the best. The young stems can also be thrown into the pot, so there's no need to handle them for preparation in any way other than washing them. See the recipe for Green Soup on page 57.

popping up all over the forest floor right now and in sheep-grazed chalky grassland, our first fungi of the year can be found – St George's mushrooms, so called because they pop up around England's national saint's day, April 23. After a weekend country walk with eagle eyes trained, foraging bag and mushroom field guide in hand to identify any specimens, we get lucky and enjoy a campfire feast of the creamy, nutty mushrooms sautéed in butter with chopped wild garlic – ambrosia.

key jobs right now

sow edible and companion flowers

Growing your own food isn't only about fruit and veg. Having flowers around is not only eye candy, for they attract pollinators that are essential for fruit-bearing plants, plus many of them are good to eat. Nasturtium seeds can be stuck anywhere in the ground or pots and produce heaps of rambling edible leaves and blindingly bright blossoms with a strong peppery bite (they can get a little unruly in midsummer and might have to be cut back). Sunflower seeds can be stuck in the ground or started in modules. A few giant ones with their plate-sized flowers create a dazzling architectural display in late summer. Wispy marigold seeds can also be sown; they are best started off in pots or modules, then transplanted once leafy to the tomato patch where they will deter whitefly. Bright blue cornflowers and borage, pansies and calendula are also edible favourites. I usually plant some sweet peas, to enjoy their beauty and as a favour to the friendly insects, but ornamental sweet peas are not to be eaten as they are poisonous! Of course I always end up with dandelions whether I like it or not. I'm not too keen on their bitter flavour, but they do make a beautiful garnish.

sow squashes This family of plants, which includes courgettes and pumpkins, need space. You can grow a courgette plant in a large 60cm diameter pot, but its sprawling tendrils will need space to spread. All parts of these plants are edible, so grow as many as you have space for. I always grow too many, but I'm madly in love with all types of squash, so what I can't use, I give away. One or two courgette plants are probably sufficient for a couple or small family, but I usually grow three or four for variety, plus several pumpkins and other slow-ripening winter squashes such as butternut, acorn and spaghetti. Sow each seed on its edge in individual pots, 2.5cm deep. Some will fail to germinate, so it's best to sow up to six of each variety.

plant artichokes Late March, April and May is the time to plant new artichoke suckers or to start them from seed (see page 35). Established plants produce suckers which are best removed for the health of the plant, so you might have a neighbour who can give you some; otherwise buy them in. They become massive plants that will need a permanent position or a giant tub.

also Sow cucumbers, as you would squashes.

'We get lucky and enjoy a campfire feast of the creamy, nutty mushrooms sautéed in butter with chopped wild garlic – ambrosia.'

Opposite An asparagus spear breaking through the soil.

late april
spring now a sure thing

I've been in a veritable frenzy of sowing and potting-on this week, now that I'm absolutely certain that winter is truly over and all danger of frost has passed. My urban habitat has not always been a safe spring haven in April. Last year my asparagus got frostbite around this time, whereas the year before, a freakishly hot month had me already exhausted by hosepipe duties and convinced I'd soon be able to grow lemons. The only certain thing about the weather is its unpredictability. One's best-laid plans must always be flexible in the veg plot.

I've decided that all my herbs are best planted at home in pots from now on, so that the odd sprig of this or that is always within arm's reach. Mint, parsley, rosemary and sage are already firmly established plants, but I'm augmenting the herbal range this week by sowing dill and coriander in their own large pots, along with two unfamiliar types: salad burnet and the rather exotic-sounding okahijiki. I also pot on some baby purple basil plants which I sowed from seed in March (see page 32). Those basil plants you buy from the supermarket never last very long, and here's why: they have a planned obsolescence. If they were everlasting, you wouldn't go back and buy another one. This is because dozens of seeds have been scattered in one pot, so due to overcrowding, the plants die off at a certain point. You can overcome this by bringing your supermarket plant home and gently separating the individual plants and giving them their own pots in which to thrive. Pinch out the top leaves, and hey presto – instant proliferation.

Back at the plot, a sunny weekend means that most of my lottie neighbours put in an appearance. Suzanne and Lloyd in Plot 4 are busy digging up their PSB. "So, it's bye-bye brassicas?" I ask. "Yep,

✳ asparagus

One of the biggest thrills of spring and a true sign that the season has arrived is the emergence of the first asparagus spear. Asparagus has a mind of its own and suddenly pops up without warning. The excitement lasts through May and part of June, but you must stop cutting it by Midsummer Day (June 24) to let it regenerate. Then, what it deprives you of in the eating, it makes up for with its display of beautiful, tall, feathery ferns through the rest of the summer.

Home-grown asparagus should be brought from the plot to the plate in as little time as possible, so wait until you are ready to cook it, then cut it an inch or two below the soil surface. The flavour is so sweet and earthy, it's almost a shame to adulterate it in any way. Steam for 3–4 minutes until bright green and tender but firm. Alternatively, brush with oil and char-grill or roast in a hot oven for 5–6 minutes. Serve with a little salt, fresh lemon juice or melted butter, or dip in a soft-boiled egg.

it's curtains I'm afraid," says Suzanne. "We need the space." She then sings the Funeral March as she carts them off in the wheelbarrow and into the skip. This will be my job in a week or so, but the bumblebees are absolutely loving my blooming brassicas, and I'm leaving the now inedible plants there as long as possible to encourage the bees to thrive, because after all, where would we be without them? And besides, the tall, luminous yellow blooms are eye candy. It does seem brutal to destroy the plants just when they seem to burst into life. But life can be like that, whatever kind of organism you are.

'One's best-laid plans must always be flexible in the veg plot.'

Top left Luminous ruby chard.
Bottom left The arch enemy, a snail on a rhubarb stalk.
Above Pepper seedings in recycled tins.

✳ rhubarb

By now, rhubarb has all but lost its pink lustre and will be heading for its greenish-brown, stringy stage in a few weeks. The flavour is still wonderful, so you can keep using it until the end of July, if you haven't decimated the plant by then – always leave 5 or 6 stalks on the plant. To harvest, pull the stalks away from the base of the plant, cut off any brown papery bits at the end of the stalk, and compost them along with the giant poisonous leaves.

A rhubarb compote or puree is a good thing to have in the freezer later in the year to flavour smoothies and desserts, or even savoury dishes where a sour edge is required (most excellent with lentils – see Rhubarb and Lentil Curry, page 75). Cut the rhubarb into 2cm pieces, and cook down with a little water and sugar to taste until completely collapsed. Cool, puree with a hand blender if desired, then pour into ice cube trays and freeze, to pop out as needed. Or, make Rhubarb Rose Eton Mess (page 56).

sow runner beans

Runners and other bean varieties can be sown now, and over the next three weeks. You can do this directly into the ground, individually in peat pots to be left on the windowsill or in the greenhouse, or in a large container (50cm plus). Runners require some configuration of tall bean poles, which can be either bamboo bought from a garden centre, or long, sturdy twigs foraged from the woods. The plants will grow to whatever height is provided, so choose your space carefully. If it's in the kitchen garden or allotment – the row should run north / south so that each side gets an equal dose of sunshine. A double row of poles works well, leaning in toward each other, crossed over and tied to another pole laid across the top. If planting directly in the soil, go ahead and build your bean frame with the poles 30cm apart, and then plant a bean at the base of each stick, 10cm deep. Alternatively, wait for the plants to develop in the peat pots in a sheltered place, and plant out later next month.

get ready for squashes and sweetcorn

Squashes, pumpkin and courgette seedlings should be well on their way now in pots in the greenhouse or on the windowsill, but there is still time to plant some if not (see page 49). You may have some pencil-thick sweetcorn plants by now too, so it's time to create a space. Squashes and sweetcorn are natural partners on the plot; the sweetcorn grows tall and the squashes sprawl out all over the place underneath them.

Native Americans traditionally grew beans in this patch as well, employing the towering sweetcorn as climbing poles, a technique known as 'Three Sisters'. I love this romantic idea, but in practice, I've only had success with the squashes and corn together – the beans always seem to get overwhelmed. Choose a square patch, as large as you can afford, dig it over now and add some compost and / or fertiliser. Aim

Left Runner bean seedlings about to be transplanted from their toilet-roll pots into the ground. **Above** Building a support frame for runner beans.

'The runner bean plants will grow to whatever height is provided, so choose your space carefully.'

to get these companion plants in the ground over the next week or two. If you are short of space, you can still have one or two squash plants, even on a balcony, training them along railings or up a trellis as they rapidly take over the space. If you do this, the fruits of large winter squashes might need some support if they are dangling from the foliage.

also Move individual tomato seedlings to intermediate pots, giving them more space to grow on indoors before planting out in their final positions in early summer.

asparagus, lentil + ricotta parcels

Here's a lovely showcase for your asparagus, wrapped in brown paper packages tied up with string – an elegant light lunch dish, served with bread and salad.

250g ricotta cheese, drained
4 heaped tbsp freshly grated Parmesan
Freshly grated zest of 1 lemon
1 clove garlic, crushed
Pinch of sea salt and freshly ground black pepper
Baking parchment, cotton string
4 rye crackers, such as Ryvita
200g cooked Puy lentils, or lentils from a tin, drained
Handful of parsley, chopped
1 heaped tbsp capers
4 spears asparagus cut in 5cm pieces, or 8 tips
Olive oil

Preheat the oven to 200°C (400°F). In a small bowl, beat together the ricotta, Parmesan, lemon zest, and crushed garlic with a pinch of salt and plenty of pepper. Rip off four pieces of baking parchment, roughly 36cm square. To assemble each parcel, break a rye cracker into a square and place in the middle of the paper. This acts as a crust and prevents the paper from getting soggy. Top with the ricotta mixture, divided evenly between each parcel. Make a slight indentation with a spoon, and top with lentils. Sprinkle with parsley and capers. Top with asparagus, and drizzle with olive oil. Bring the corners of the paper together, scrunch and tie with cotton string. Place on a baking tray and cook for about 15 minutes, until warmed through. Serve with bread and salad.

Serves 4

Prep tip Hold the cut end of each asparagus with one hand and the middle of the spear with the other and bend until it snaps. The breaking point should be where the tough part of the spear ends. I always have a nibble on the broken-off ends – they can be coarse, but freshly cut asparagus is an unmissable treat raw.

rhubarb rose
eton mess

Here the mysterious perfume of rosewater meets rhubarb's quirky tartness, suspended in pillows of cream and crunchy meringue. Rosewater differs vastly in potency from brand to brand. It can be found in Middle Eastern grocery stores if not the supermarket, and I usually opt for a Lebanese version, but any variety will do.

300g rhubarb, trimmed weight (about 2 thick stalks), sliced
75g caster sugar
4 store-bought individual meringue nests
300ml double cream
1–2 tbsp rosewater, or to taste

Place the rhubarb and sugar in a saucepan over a medium heat and cover. When the sugar melts and it starts to boil, stir, lower the heat to a simmer and cook uncovered for 10 minutes, stirring once or twice. Remove to a heat-proof bowl and leave to cool completely, then chill.

When ready to serve, crumble the meringues into a bowl, leaving them in a few bite-size chunks. Whip the cream until it holds it shape and forms soft peaks, but do not over-whip so that it is stiff. Add the rosewater, starting with 1 tbsp, and beat briefly until thick again. Taste and add more rosewater if you think it needs it – the flavour should be subtle but recognisable. Stir the cream mixture through the meringues, then fold through the rhubarb so it is streaky but not evenly combined. Spoon into glasses and serve as soon as possible, though it will sit happily for half an hour or so. (Alternatively, construct each portion with layers of meringue, cream, and rhubarb in each glass.) **Serves 4**

Prep tip Bright pink, young, early rhubarb gives this dessert the best colour, but you can use any rhubarb right up to the end of the season in July.

green soup

Fill about a third of a carrier bag full of edible greens for this soup, including young nettle tips, rocket, chard, sorrel, and lettuce. Grab some chive flowers and dandelions to garnish.

2 tbsp virgin rapeseed oil or
  olive oil
4 spring onions, sliced
3 leeks, roughly chopped
500g potatoes, washed
  but not peeled, cut into
  2cm cubes

Sea salt
1 litre vegetable stock
150g garden greens, washed
  and roughly chopped
Juice of half a lemon
Freshly ground black pepper
Double cream, to serve

Heat a soup pan over a medium heat and add the oil. Add the spring onions, leeks and potato with a little sea salt. Stir, cover and cook for 5 minutes, stirring frequently.

Add the stock and bring to the boil. Stir and simmer for 10 minutes, or until the potato is soft. Add the greens and simmer for a further 3–5 minutes to cook the greens. Cool briefly, then puree with a hand blender until completely smooth. Taste for seasoning, then squeeze in a little lemon juice and grind in some pepper. Serve each bowl with a drizzle of cream and more pepper.
Serves 4–6

Prep tip Be sure to wear gloves when picking nettles. Choose baby nettles or young tips, avoiding any woody-stemmed specimens. Keep the gloves on when you rinse them, but don't bother to chop.

foolproof hollandaise

This easy, indulgent sauce is made in the blender and goes perfectly with asparagus and PSB.

Place 3 organic egg yolks in a blender jar with 2 tbsp water and 1 tbsp lemon juice (don't blend yet). Melt 150g salted butter. Start blending the eggs and pour the hot butter throught the hole in the lid until you have a thick and creamy emulsion. Serve immediately. (It solidifies once cold, but can be reheated in a microwave.)

MAY	INDOORS OR UNDER GLASS	OUTDOORS DIRECT IN SOIL
Asparagus		
Beetroot		★
Broad beans		★
Broccoli (calabrese)	★	★
Broccoli (sprouting)	★	★
Brussel sprouts	★	★
Cabbage (spring)		
Cabbage (summer/winter)	★	★
Carrots		★
Cauliflower	★	★
Celeriac	★	★
Chard	★	★
Courgettes	★	★
Cucumbers	★	
Elderflowers		
Fennel	★	
Flowers (edible/companion)	★	★
Globe artichokes		★
Grape leaves		
Kale	★	★
Lettuce/salad leaves	★	★
Nettles		
Parnsips		★
Pea shoots		
Peas	★	★
Peppers and chillies		
Perpetual spinach	★	★
Potatoes		★
Radishes	★	★
Rhubarb	★	
Rocket		★
Runner beans/other beans	★	★
Salsify/scorzonera	★	★
Spinach	★	★
Spring herbs	★	★
Spring onions	★	★
Squashes/pumpkins	★	★
Strawberries		★
Summer herbs	★	★
Swedes	★	★
Sweetcorn		★
Tomatoes	★	★
Turnips		★
Winter herbs		★

UITABLE FOR CONTAINERS	HARVESTING NOW	RECIPES AND OTHER INFORMATION
★	★	asparagus, lentil + ricotta parcels, 55; *see also 50*
★		*see 138*
★	★	broad bean tabbouleh, 92; *see also 68, 75, 112*
★		*see 98*
★	★	psb + barley risotto, 39; *see also 35*
★		zesty brussels sprouts, 203; *see also 27, 42, 195*
★	★	lemony lentil cabbage parcels, 203; *see also 123*
★		hot + sour swede + cabbage salad, 200
★		*see 167, 179*
★	★	cauliflower + coconut soup, 182; *see 172, 183*
★		celeriac gratin + ceps, 182, *see also 175*
★	★	sorrel + chard kuku, 36; *see also 32, 39, 57*
★		warm courgette salad, 113; *see also 102, 128, 148*
★		smoky gazpacho, 128; *see also 105, 167*
	★	elderflower cordial, 74; *see also 70, 75*
★		*see 140*
★		*see 116*
		ultimate artichoke, 94; *see also 80, 93*
	★	*see 87*
★	★	saffron rice broth + winter greens, 38; *see also 42*
★	★	broad beans with lettuce, 75; *see also 57, 63*
	★	green soup, 57; *see also 48*
★		parsnip, pear + stilton soup, 202; *see also 193*
★	★	*see 67*
★	★	pea + feta egg cups, 72; *see also 67*
★		*see 112, 131, 143, 144*
★	★	*see 32*
★		parmesan potato cakes, 93; *see also 57, 91*
★	★	*see 64*
	★	rhubarb + lentil curry, 75; *see also 52, 56*
★	★	green soup, 57; *see 46*
★		soy glazed runner beans, 112; *see also 106, 127, 131*
★		*see 190*
★	★	*see 32*
★	★	sorrel + chard kuku, 36; *see also 31, 57*
★	★	green soup, 57; *see also 61, 72, 92, 112, 131*
★		pumpkin pasty, 169; *see also 124, 149, 162, 165, 167*
★		*see 83*
★	★	parmesan potato cakes, 93; *see also 28, 84*
★		hot + sour swede + cabbage salad, 200; *see also 197*
★		sweetcorn + spiced avocado soup, 131; *see also 119*
★		slow-roasted tomatoes, 131; *see also 120, 158, 166*
★	★	*see 180*
★	★	*see 150, 169, 198*

early may
the hungry gap

May is defined by asparagus for me. Every day I return from the plot with a small clutch of thick, juicy, and usually wonky spears that would never make it past the supermarket inspectors. I steam it right away and have it from the plot to the plate in less than 20 minutes. Asparagus really is the food of the gods, my desert-island vegetable, its sweetness incomparable even to the freshest farm asparagus which is available all over the place right now.

This daily asparagus dose, 4–6 spears a day usually, is provided by just four asparagus crowns that I planted in my first year at the allotment. Asparagus can be a bit fussy, so I took advice to plant one-year-old crowns in April rather than grow from seed. The asparagus bed is a permanent position of productivity for up to 20 years, and now I wish I'd planted more than four, as I could happily double my daily consumption.

Not just because I love it so, but because there's not a fat lot else to eat at the moment! It's such an odd time of the year in the garden – The Hungry Gap. Despite a swathe of botanical exuberance all over the plot and on the windowsill at home, with everything seemingly doubling in size daily (weeds included), it's all just coming to life but has a way to go before it's edible. There's a sensation of "Food, food everywhere, but not a bite to eat". It's a rather counter-intuitive situation I've only really grasped since becoming an urban farmer. You can gently coerce Nature, but you can't be in the driver's seat.

So for the last couple of weeks, I've been eating out more than usual, or surviving mostly on asparagus and rhubarb, and relying on last year's crops from the freezer, for which I'm most grateful. It's a good idea to step up the pace of using up freezer produce right now regardless, to make room for the imminent onslaught.

✳ spring onions

Just about any young onion can be enjoyed in its entirety – green parts and all – before it is fully developed, but special varieties of salad onion are well worth growing, as they are quick, trouble-free and essential in summer salads.

Spring onions are lovely lightly fried and added to scrambled eggs or omelettes, alone or with cheese, tomatoes and fresh garden herbs. They store for an amazingly long time in a jug of water in the kitchen – just change the water every few days. If you have a surplus, they can be left to mature into bigger bulbs, or chopped and frozen in bags, ready to toss into the frying pan or wok.

Opposite New asparagus pops up seemingly overnight, pictured here with some of the stumps of last year's cut stalks.

sow summer and autumn root crops

Root vegetable seeds invariably prefer to be sown directly in the ground, or in large pots for the patio; the point being that once sown, they must be left to develop in their final position. Carrots and beetroot are fine to grow in deep pots. If you haven't prepared a space yet in the kitchen garden or allotment, clear and dig it now. Be sure to use a space where you haven't grown roots last year or where the soil hasn't been manured the previous year, otherwise your roots may turn into multi-pronged 'Frankenveg'. Most root crops are planted in shallow drills about 15cm apart, but just follow seed packet instructions for sowing.

If sowing long, deep root crops, especially parsnips, scorzonera or salsify, the ground will need to be as

Above Potato flowers indicate the tubers may be ready to dig up and eat.

stone-free as possible, so you may need to sift it to get a decent crop. This is an undeniably boring and labour-intensive job, which you may think is hardly worth it for a crop that can be cheaply bought at the supermarket. But shop-bought root veg will never taste as sweet or give you the pleasure of watching the crop come to fruition over the coming months. I grow a round, stubby variety of carrots that overcomes the problem of my dense clay soil, and I grow a few baby crops in pots at home too. I've found that beetroot is quite happy growing in my dense soil.

Beetroot and carrots can be sown successionally over the summer months for a continuous supply. Parsnips, scorzonera and salsify take months to develop and can sit in the soil for ages, so they can be sown now once and for all. Be sure to thin out the seedlings once they are large enough to handle, to give each vegetable enough space to develop. The thinnings are edible and tasty, so wash them and throw them in a salad.

wild potatoes – enjoy and destroy

No matter how hard I try to harvest every single potato, a few always remain in the soil and start coming up in last year's potato bed, which might now be full of broad beans or brassicas, and even some from several years past too in other areas. The easily recognisable leaves can be pulled out as weeds, but if some are popping up in a space where they're not interfering, why not let them grow until they reveal some small potatoes beneath? Well, the conventional wisdom is that they should be pulled up immediately as they have the potential to spread disease. It's an added bonus to have a few tasty little microspuds this early in the year, but I'll leave it to you to decide whether you want to risk it.

also Earth up potatoes. Keep covering the leaves of your new crop with soil to encourage strong tubers.

Sow bulb fennel seeds in a pot on the windowsill or in a greenhouse for a late summer / early autumn crop.

 lettuce

By now, a tray of baby lettuce leaves or even full heads may well be ready to eat. It's a great joy when salad days are here again. You can even grow baby leaves indors In winter. Remember to keep sowing fast-growing lettuce little and often – every two or three weeks in a tray to be planted out or eaten young, snipped from the windowsill. A mixture of your own freshly cut leaves is infinitely superior and cheaper than what's available to buy.

All lettuce, especially the hearting varieties such as Cos, cook beautifully. Cook any lettuce leaves with broad beans (see page 75), or braise whole hearts with wine, stock, butter and sprigs of winter herbs. Due to its high water content, lettuce works well in soup, either cooked in a hot soup, or pureed raw with yoghurt, lemon, mint and garlic and chilled for a cooling summer treat. Bolted lettuces will ooze a bitter milky substance when cut, so they'll be heading straight for the compost bin – this substance is also a narcotic.

radishes

The first radishes should be ready to eat just under three weeks from sowing, and you can keep on sowing them throughout the summer for near instant gratification, as they are so quick growing.

Pink breakfast radishes add a welcome splash of colour to salads before tomatoes arrive on the scene, and they are also delicious dipped into soft salted butter, French-style. There are dozens of varieties – I've been growing a white Asian variety which expands to enormous proportions if I let it, getting hotter and spicier all the time. These larger varieties can be grated or julienned and mixed into a delicious salad seasoned with rice vinegar, light soy sauce, sugar, dried chilli flakes, spring onions and toasted sesame seeds.

Radishes are more versatile than you might think – they can be roasted, sautéed, stir-fried or stewed in curries or tagines, though I think they taste best raw. Radishes are one of the few veg that doesn't freeze well, but can be pickled.

mid-may
crushing defeat

Every living thing on the plot is responding to rising temperatures and spring showers with orgiastic enthusiasm. I start to wonder where the fine line is between devotion and obsession, as I've recently turned down dinner invitations to put in the evening hours on the plot, and edible plants are featuring nightly in my dreams. It is possible for allotmenteering to be simply a part-time hobby, but I've really fallen for it. I can't help but get emotionally attached to the plants I bring to life, cheering them on when they approach maturity, thanking them when they bear fruit, and relishing every home-grown mouthful of the harvest. But that journey isn't without its hardships – trying to coax life back into plants when they are struck by disease or pests or hailstones. Or just plain feeling guilty if I don't have time for them.

After a short trip away and hence a three-day absence from the plot, I'm not too worried as there has been some rain and slug defences have been mounted in the form of coffee grounds and beer traps. Nevertheless, I find myself racing back to see what changes are afoot.

I'm shocked to see that my rhubarb plant has sprung a humongous flower as big as me! As this hasn't ever happened before, I'm not sure whether to jump for joy or reach for the machete. After a quick spot of internet research, the verdict is clear: off with its head. As in many cases, the flower diverts the plant's energy and should be removed to prolong its productivity. I've had just about all the rhubarb I can handle this year, but I'll keep it going a while longer and certainly do whatever is necessary to maintain the health of this plant, which should have up to a ten-year lifespan. So I yank the huge flower off from the base, using the strength of both arms, and haul it over to the compost bin.

Then, I have a moment of despair when I open the greenhouse to find that three of my carefully nurtured baby aubergine seedlings have been completely devoured by a snail. I find the culprit languishing guiltlessly in the corner of the greenhouse, and I'm afraid my anger-fueled reaction was, well – you crush me, I crush you, you slimeball! At least on the urban farm I don't have rabbits or deer to contend with. If only there was some sporting way of eliminating these infuriating molluscs, I'd play the game. Instead, I dispose of the snail that has met its maker and, despite my best efforts to be as organic and wildlife friendly as possible, I reluctantly reach for the slug pellets in a quick-fix attempt to save the few remaining aubergines.

Elsewhere on the plot, the last of the winter crops have finally bitten the dust – I pull up all the blooming brassicas and bolted leeks and chard and compost what I can. Alas, rotation, rotation. This clearance may be a little overdue by some people's standards, but the plants weren't doing any harm, especially to the bees, who were enjoying the brassica flowers to the end.

Disposing of the brassicas is no simple task. I must be burning some serious calories as I wrestle with ten purple sprouting broccoli plants, most bigger than me, that have to be dug up and man-handled into the skip. Traditionally, certain stems of these often behemoth plants were stripped, dried, varnished and used to make walking sticks, so the stem is a bit too hard core for the compost heap, but I strip as much foliage as I have the patience to remove and compost that. It's sad to see these old reliable winter crops go, but as one door closes, another opens…

'If only there was some sporting way of eliminating these infuriating molluscs, I'd play the game.'

Above There's no mercy when it comes to snails on my beloved veg.

'By nipping off the top 15cm of any broad bean plants around flowering time, you might well stop the blackfly in their tracks.'

Above left Broad bean blossom and a young pod.
Above right A clutch of rocket seed pods ready to hang to dry.

pinch out broad bean tops

Blackfly will be an inevitable nuisance on your broad beans; they'll colonise on the tips of the plants early on in their life, usually around the flowering stage. It's the tender tips of the plant they are after. If left to carry on, blackfly can result in a poor yield, a revolting infestation and even the destruction of the crop completely. By nipping off the top 15cm of any broad bean plants around flowering time, you might well stop the blackfly in their tracks. These tender tops are delicious steamed, sautéed or stir-fried.

harvest pea shoots

Once pea plants are about 15cm tall, snip off the top set of leaves and any accompanying tendrils. This will encourage the plant to throw out more shoots. Enjoy this first small harvest in salads, then carry on snipping the 5cm to 13cm shoots every three weeks or so. Once they turn tough and bitter, leave this plant and move on to younger plants for more shoots.

hang rocket for seed

Any rocket that has stuck around since winter will now surely have gone to seed, and this may happen several times a year if you sow it successionally as I do. If you deem your rocket to be a healthy and successful strain, you can regenerate it easily by simply cutting the stems with seed pods, tying them together and hanging them upside down in a dry place such as a shed or kitchen window. Once completely dry, hold the stalks over a large bowl and crush the dry pods between your fingertips to release the seeds. The seed and chaff will sink to the bottom of the bowl. Discard the stem and pick out and discard or compost the seed pods. Store the seeds in an airtight container and keep sowing in the ground, trays, pots or window boxes. Tasty, nutritious food for free!

also Plant runner bean seedlings or sow seeds directly in the ground (see page 52).

peas and shoots

The earliest peas take about 11 weeks to start cropping, so it may be too soon to enjoy the peas themselves. However, pea shoots are a flavourful salad ingredient, with a distinctive flavour reminiscent of pea pods. They can be ready to eat after sowing in a very short time (see left).

Your pea crop will peak later this month or in June, and can be carried on through the summer with successional sowing if it's not too hot. I can't resist eating them raw straight from the pod, or with pod and all when they are at the 'mangetout' stage.

Achieving a sizeable batch of podded peas is a time-consuming affair. I usually enjoy small, fresh batches, just steamed or raw and thrown into salads. If you can't eat them right away, just freeze them, out of the pod and raw. The empty pods can be made into soup which will have to be pureed and strained but tastes sweet and light. The pods can also be made into wine, if you are so inclined.

late may
closing the gap

Each day I've been impatiently eyeing up the swelling peas and broad bean pods in anticipation – once you can make out their curvy shapes inside the pods, they should be ready to eat. Everything else is still in its infancy. It's a time of nurturing now, putting in the hours in the lengthening evenings to coax the summer bounty. The strawberries are just starting to blush and currants are fat but green. Pre-pubescent tomato plants are gathering momentum in pots and showing yellow flowers, and a few baby artichokes are emerging. The asparagus has slowed down to a couple of spears a day, but there's still rhubarb a-plenty.

So, if there's not much to eat in the garden or on the plot right now, head for the hedgerow! Elderflowers are starting to kick off all over the city, and not just in the capital's green spaces. I've seen them hanging over bus stops and brick walls at just about every turn, sagging with the weight of their heady blossom and filling the air with a strong perfume. Some indulgent fritters are always on the menu this time of year (see page 75).

The greenhouse is bursting at the seams with happy seedlings, including heat-loving peppers and chillies and what survived of my aubergines. I recorded a temperature of 45°C in the heat of the day recently, so ventilation is paramount. This makeshift greenhouse, which my husband Dan and I built from some discarded plastic sheeting we found in the woods, has been a godsend for raising young plants in cool weather, since we long ago ran out of space on our windowsill at home. Splashing out on new greenhouse has never seemed in the spirit of our allotment efforts, where we try to reuse, recycle, spend the minimum and reduce our carbon footprint. If a greenhouse is out of the question for you, consider this: have you got a car? Someone in our neighbourhood is using

✳ broad beans

The arrival of the first broad beans is cause for celebration – it's a drum roll for the kick-off of the summer harvest. An early crop will almost certainly have been planted in late autumn and, though extremely slow to develop, it means a crop as early as May, with more to come through the early summer if you planted a spring crop in March.

When cooking them plain, I prefer to steam broad beans, just for 3–5 minutes depending on size. Lightly steamed, they marry well with Parmesan, lemon, garlic and olive oil. All parts of the plant are edible, including the pods – tastier when young – and the leaf tops can be steamed or sautéed in butter. Empty pods can be rinsed and boiled to make vegetable stock.

Mature broad beans can be dried and stored, then soaked overnight and cooked. In this guise they become a different animal altogether – rich, brown and buttery. In Egypt they are called ful medames and are eaten warm with garlic, lemon, olive oil and hard-boiled egg.

Left Pick elderflowers just before you are ready to cook them. **Above right** Romano pepper plants soon to be transplanted to their final positions. **Above** Placing straw under the strawberries protects them from ground-dwelling pests.

'Elderflowers are starting to kick off all over the city, and not just in the capital's green spaces.'

their Volvo estate as a greenhouse. Chock full of plants, it moves around regularly, so it's still being used as a car. While I can't say how 'green' such a greenhouse actually is, this practical alternative use is clearly offsetting the environmental impact of the vehicle to some degree.

At last, the first clutch of the overwintering broad beans, planted last November, are ready to be popped out of their fuzzy casings. They are barely the size of my thumbnail, but it's time to steam the first few handfuls of the season. This means it's official – The Hungry Gap is now closed. Hooray!

✳ elderflowers

Cream-coloured clusters of elderflower pop out all over the South of England as early as late May for a few weeks. In cooler parts of the UK, this wonderful wild food may not be ready until mid-June. Once you know what to look for, you'll start seeing them everywhere, as the trees, which sometimes resemble giant bushes, are adaptable even to urban environments.

It's tempting to grab a bouquet to take home, but a word of warning: after a few hours or less, the cut blossoms throw out a strong, house-filling odour that is uncannily like cat pee. Avoid this at all costs. Identify your bush, choose your recipe, gather your other ingredients, and only then set off with a bag and scissors for your elderflower foraging. Aim to return to process them immediately. Snip off clusters which smell fresh. Head straight back to the kitchen and cook.

Elderflowers are famously good with gooseberries, which should be arriving on the scene at about the same time.

key jobs right now

protect soft fruits As your strawberries, raspberries and currants start to blush pink and red, the birds will make a bee-line for them, so it's time to protect the plants and bushes with netting. This can be crudely but effectively done by driving posts or sticks in four corners around the fruit. Place a plastic cup or bottle over the stakes and drape a net over them. Secure at the bottom with stones, bricks or tent pegs.

get ready for the fruit and veg tsunami
With The Hungry Gap now closed, unless you have been highly calculated and judicious, this is the start of a continuous and sometimes overwhelming period of harvesting. Make room in the freezer, arm yourself with small, medium and large resealable bags, and keep collecting empty jars with metal lids for preserves.

also Plant out bean, sweetcorn and squash plants to their final positions.

Opposite Netting over the berry patch, suspended over a plastic bottle on a stake, keeps birds off the fruit.

pea + feta egg cups

These can practically be thrown together with your eyes closed, once the peas are shelled – perfect for lazy weekend breakfasts, or multiply for a brunch buffet. Serve hot with toasted baguette rounds or cold either on their own or with salad.

2 spring onions, chopped
200g peas (shelled weight)
3 large organic eggs, beaten
75g feta cheese, crumbled
2 tbsp single cream
Handful of fresh mint leaves, chopped
Sea salt and freshly ground black pepper

A non-stick muffin tin, with 6 well-greased holes

Toasted baguette slices to serve (optional)

Preheat the oven to 200°C (400°F).

Combine all the ingredients in a bowl or pouring jug and mix well.

Pour the mixture into the muffin holes, filling to just below the top edge to allow for expansion. Bake for 15–20 minutes, until puffed and golden. Serve hot or cold.
Makes 6

Prep tip If you don't have enough fresh peas, supplement the weight with frozen ones, or use all frozen – just run them under a hot tap to defrost them first.

elderflower cordial

Here's how you can hang onto that glorious taste of early summer for months to come, as a refreshing drink diluted with cold fizzy or still water. It's also excellent in cocktails or dribbled over vanilla ice cream. Citric acid powder acts as a preservative for the cordial and gives it a sharp flavour. If you can't find it in a pharmacy, look in Asian food shops – it's usually with the spices, and will probably be cheaper there as well. You'll also find it in shops where wine-making equipment is sold.

20 heads of elderflower
  (or a few more if small)
2 large unwaxed lemons,
  sliced
1.5 litres water
65g citric acid powder
  (available at pharmacies)
1.75kg caster sugar
5 empty 500ml plastic water
  or milk bottles with caps,
  cleaned

Inspect the elderflower heads and brush off any insects. Place in a large ceramic bowl with the lemon slices.

Measure the water into a saucepan and place over a high heat to bring to the boil. Put the citric acid and sugar in a separate large saucepan, ladle in some of the measured water, and heat gently to dissolve, stirring frequently. Pour the boiling water over the elderflowers and lemons. Add the sugar and citric acid solution and give it a gentle stir. Mix well.

Cool completely, stir again, cover and leave in a cool place for 5 days out of the light, stirring well morning and night.

Strain the big stuff through a fine-ish sieve into a large pouring jug. Stretch a muslin, cheesecloth or nylon stocking (I keep a pack of unused knee-highs in the kitchen – they're handy) over a funnel so it's tight around the edges but a little loose in the middle. Place the funnel over a smaller jug. Pour the sieve-strained cordial through the funnel for crystal-clear and bug-free cordial, then pour carefully into five clean 500ml plastic bottles, leaving a little empty space at the top for freezer expansion. Screw on the caps. Store in a cool, dark place or in the freezer, where it will keep indefinitely. Once opened, keep in the fridge. To serve, dilute with still or sparkling water. Makes just over 2 litres of cordial.

rhubarb + lentil curry

Rhubarb in a curry may sound bizarre, but its sharpness marries beautifully with lentils and spices. Once you tire of rhubarb desserts, this makes a refreshing savoury change.

2 tbsp virgin rapeseed oil or
   sunflower oil
2 leeks, trimmed and sliced
1 medium onion, chopped
2 celery stalks, sliced
3 cloves garlic (remove the
   bitter sprout from the
   middle, if old)
1 tsp cumin seed
1 tsp coriander seed
½ tsp coarse crystal sea salt
2 tsp paprika

¼ tsp turmeric
350g rhubarb, cut into 1cm
   chunks (about 2–3 thick or
   6–8 thin stalks)
150g Puy lentils
700ml vegetable stock
1–2 tbsp dark brown sugar
Sea salt and freshly ground
   black pepper
Boiled basmati rice, thick
   natural yoghurt and fresh
   coriander leaves or parsley,
   to serve

Heat a large pan over a medium heat and add the oil. Add the leeks, onion, and celery and cook, stirring frequently, until soft.

Meanwhile, place the garlic, cumin, coriander seed and ½ tsp coarse salt in a mortar and pound the garlic to a paste. Add this mixture to the pan with the softened leeks, along with the paprika and turmeric, and stir for about a minute, until fragrant. Next add the rhubarb, lentils and stock, cover and bring to the boil.

Reduce the heat to a simmer and cook for half an hour. Add 1 tbsp brown sugar and taste the liquid in the pan. Adjust the seasoning, adding salt and pepper and more sugar if necessary. Leave the pan uncovered and simmer for a further 30 minutes, stirring occasionally.

Serve on a bed of cooked basmati rice, with a dollop of yoghurt and fresh herbs scattered over each bowl.
Serves 4–6

Prep tip Compost the poisonous rhubarb leaves. A gentle brush helps to clean the rhubarb stalks if they are mud-specked.

elderflower fritters

An incredibly indulgent treat – use the flower heads ASAP after picking.

Simply inspect the heads for insects and shake them off. Make a light batter with self-raising flour, cold fizzy water or sparkling cider, an egg and a touch of sugar, to make a medium-thick consistency. Heat a shallow pool of sunflower oil in a large frying pan, dip the heads in the batter holding the stem end, and fry until crisp and golden. Dredge with icing sugar and devour.

broad beans with lettuce

My favourite way to cook broad beans, especially early ones, is steamed with its spring partner on the plot, lettuce

Line a saucepan with lettuce leaves. Add a knob of salted butter, wet your hand and sprinkle a few drops of water in. Add the beans, cover and place over a moderate heat. The lettuce will collapse and release a delicate steam which cooks the beans, and the cooked lettuce tastes delicious as well. .

summer

JUNE	INDOORS OR UNDER GLASS	OUTDOORS DIRECT IN SO
Asparagus		
Baby new potatoes		
Beetroot		★
Broad beans		
Broccoli (calabrese)		
Broccoli (sprouting)		★
Cabbage (summer)		
Cabbage (spring/winter)	★	★
Carrots		★
Cauliflower	★	★
Celeriac	★	★
Chard	★	★
Cherries		
Courgettes	★	★
Cucumbers	★	★
Elderflowers		
Fennel	★	★
Flowers (edible/companion)	★	★
Garlic		
Globe artichokes		
Grape leaves		
Kale	★	★
Lettuce/salad leaves	★	★
Pea shoots	★	★
Peas		★
Perpetual spinach	★	★
Radishes	★	★
Rhubarb		
Rocket	★	★
Runner beans/other beans		★
Spinach	★	★
Spring onions		★
Squashes/pumpkins	★	★
Strawberries		★
Summer berries		
Summer herbs	★	★
Swede		★
Sweetcorn	★	★
Turnips		★
Winter herbs	★	★

UITABLE FOR CONTAINERS	HARVESTING NOW	RECIPES AND OTHER INFORMATION
★	★	asparagus, lentil + ricotta parcels, 55; *see also 50*
★	★	*see 91*
★	★	*see 138*
★	★	broad bean tabbouleh, 92; *see also 68, 75, 112*
★	★	*see 98*
★		psb + barley risotto, 39; *see also 35*
★	★	lemony lentil cabbage parcels, 203; *see also 123*
★		hot + sour swede + cabbage salad, 200
★	★	*see 167, 179*
★	★	cauliflower + coconut soup, 182; *see 172, 183*
★		celeriac gratin + ceps, 182, *see also 175*
★	★	sorrel + chard kuku, 36; *see also 32, 39, 57*
★	★	*see 89*
★		warm courgette salad, 113; *see also 102, 128, 148*
★	★	smoky gazpacho, 128; *see also 105, 167*
	★	elderflower cordial, 74; *see also 70, 75*
★		*see 140*
★	★	*see 116*
★	★	broad bean + garlic purée; *see also 39, 55, 75, 100*
	★	ultimate artichoke, 94; *see also 80, 93,*
★	★	see 87
★	★	saffron rice broth + winter greens, 38; *see also 42*
★	★	broad beans with lettuce, 75; *see also 57, 63*
★	★	*see 67*
★	★	pea + feta egg cups, 72; *see also 67*
★	★	*see 32*
★	★	*see 64*
	★	rhubarb + lentil curry, 75; *see also 52, 56*
★	★	green soup, 57; *see 46*
★	★	soy glazed runner beans, 112; *see also 106, 127, 131*
★	★	*see 32*
★	★	green soup, 57; *see also 61, 72, 92, 112, 131*
★		pumpkin pasty, 169; *see also 124, 149, 162, 165, 167*
★	★	*see 83*
★	★	*see 108*
★	★	parmesan potato cakes, 93; *see also 28, 84*
★		hot + sour swede + cabbage salad, 200; *see also 197*
★		sweetcorn + spiced avocado soup, 131; *see also 119*
★	★	*see 180*
★	★	*see 150, 169, 198*

early june
potting on apace

I can sense an imminent eruption of colour on the lottie. What was a pure verdant panel is now transitioning into a palette of reds, yellows and pinks, as the berries ripen and blossoms appear on squashes, potatoes, tomatoes and nasturtiums.

I pick and duly wolf down my first few handfuls of sun-warmed strawberries on the first day of June, a fitting date, as these fruits personify the month. Every evening recently we've had a small-scale feast of peas and broad beans, mint, coriander and pea shoot-laced salads, as well as baby artichokes.

Suddenly, everything needs planting out or potting on, especially the trays of lettuces and the brassicas in the greenhouse, so I've been working hard to get things moved to their final positions, which means first preparing the spaces, clearing the weeds and raking the stones, shards of concrete, brick and pottery that constantly wash to the surface when it rains. My plot was a bomb site in World War II and often some rather poignant relics resurface after rain or digging – a tiny jar of Bovril, a rusty watch, an oyster shell fragment, a key. Of course, there's always rubbish to clear away that blows in from the street or gets deliberately thrown in, which always baffles me.

Much of my time is currently being devoted to weed control. Young weed sprouts, when caught early and if space allows, simply need to be razed with a sharp hoe. Just a few days' lapse without the hoe and it's back to hand-weeding. It's impossible to hoe the onion patch without destroying the onions, and although the onions don't seem to mind the weeds that much, the weeds spiral out of control seemingly overnight.

It takes me two hours to clear the avenues of weeds between the alliums, with gloved hands and

✳ globe artichokes

If you planted your artichokes this year, resist cutting them until next. Once plants are established, you'll be loving this time of the season for years to come. Don't hesitate to cut the chokes when still babies; this encourages the plant to produce more. On smaller plants, cut the 'king head' or main central choke first. Artichokes invariably harbour insects, especially blackfly, so soak them in water dosed with vinegar; the bugs will make a swift exit.

Full instructions on how to prepare artichokes are given on page 94. Young artichokes can be eaten raw (see the Artichoke Carpaccio recipe on page 93).

If you want to freeze the hearts, follow the instructions given on page 94, cool and freeze in labelled bags.

'Young weed sprouts, when caught early and if space allows, just need to be razed with a sharp hoe. Just a few days' lapse without the hoe and it's back to hand-weeding.'

a hand hoe. Weeding can be an almost meditative act, but the back of my thighs are really suffering from bending over for so long.

In the root vegetable patch, areas of sowings directly in the ground from a few weeks ago have to be left with weeds flourishing until I'm able to distinguish the feathery carrot fronds, the pink-tinged teardrop beetroot leaves and the parsley-shaped parsnip sprouts from the surrounding uninvited guests. This is a feat of patience, which demands a discerning eye, but once the initial clearing is accomplished, the desired seedlings can then be thinned out, and the root veg will start to progress visibly in leaps and bounds.

key jobs right now

Below Nip off side shoots where leaves meet the main stem on cordon variety tomatoes.

plant tomatoes in their final positions and prune

Choose a sunny and fairly sheltered area for your outdoor tomatoes to be planted out. This can be done as early as May if the weather is sufficiently warm. Tomatoes turn into huge plants, so give them plenty of room – space them about 60cm apart or more. Alternatively, raise them in grow bags or large pots.

Cordon, or 'indeterminate' varieties can be easily trained, but will need sturdy support provided by stakes or a frame of thick bamboo or sticks, erected as for runner beans (see pages 52–53). This is best done now but can wait a bit longer if necessary, as long as they have some temporary support, such as a small cane. These varieties need control for the best crop, so keep nipping off any side shoots that form in the crux where the leaves meet the main stem (see left); cut with secateurs if they have become large. Even if you have let some of these stems get very large, don't worry, just prune them back rather brutally to one main stem – in my experience they always recover. Larger shoots will turn into whole new plants if you stand them in water, ideally in a can or opaque container to encourage new roots to form. This is best done early in the season so any cuttings have time to develop into yet more of these remarkable plants, which can then be planted out. Bush varieties don't need pruning, but they need plenty of room between them for aeration. A bed of straw underneath will help save ground level fruits from slugs.

Once the first flowers have set on the tomato plants and no earlier, you can start feeding them with a liquid tomato feed. Keep this up every two weeks or so. Mark on a calendar each time you do it (I've got a calendar pinned up inside my shed), so you don't forget.

plant out leeks

Leeks can go in the patch with the other alliums – just remember they will probably be there much longer than the rest of the family, well into winter or even next spring. The common advice is to plant out leeks when they are 'pencil thickness', but I find they plant out just fine even if they are only chive-size. The key is to make 15cm-deep holes about 15cm apart with the end of a broom handle or trowel handle, drop the leek seedlings in, gently fill the holes with water, and they will soon settle in. If you've got more seedlings than space to plant out, cook and eat them now (snip into salads or fry like spring onions), or plant them in a cluster; they won't mature properly but they'll stay alive and you can eat them whenever you're ready or even plant them out later.

also Pot on cucumbers, peppers and aubergines into their final large pots. Peppers and aubergines will do best in a greenhouse, but cucumbers, if an outdoor variety, will be happy outside (see page 87).

strawberries

Strawberries are simple to grow but, once they sweeten and turn red, slugs will get to them before you have a chance and, if you haven't protected your patch with netting, so will the birds. Placing straw under ripening fruits will deter slugs and other ground-dwelling pests.

Enjoy your daily harvest for breakfast with muesli or yoghurt and honey. Or stuff a blender full of berries, top with vanilla ice cream and whiz for the ultimate strawberry milkshake. My favourite strawberry dessert is a mix of berries, crushed meringues and whipped cream flavoured with rosewater (see also the rhubarb version on page 56). The leaves and blossoms are a gorgeous garnish for strawberry-themed desserts.

Jam making is the obvious use for a quantity of berries, however I prefer to eat a fresh portion each day in June. Any excess can be washed, hulled and frozen in smallish quantities in labelled bags to use straight from the freezer in breakfast smoothies or plopped into a glass of bubbly.

mid-june
solstice bounty

Ahh, bliss. It's payback time. These long, warm days are our reward for getting through the dark winter weeks way back when. Everything, weeds included, shoot up twofold in a week. Runner beans race up the poles, sweetcorn is a foot high, squashes sprawl every which way, and broad beans and strawberries positively gush. My weeknight routine, once I've finished work, is a relentless pattern of weeding, watering, reaping, washing, trimming, shelling, cooking and eating. Dinner is always late, as I'm usually beavering away in the midsummer evening light til 10pm. Sometimes, I'm so knackered when I get back, I fall into bed with an empty belly. All this for probably more food than our household can get through, but such a labour of love is worth every backache and certainly every mouthful.

With lots of young plants out, especially lettuces, I try a new slug trap: a watermelon rind. A friend in the USA tells me she leaves the rinds out at night and slugs and snails collect on them – then she incinerates them in the morning for revenge! Certainly worth a try, as Greek watermelons are in season and available from my local shop right now. Though as I'm a bit squeamish, I'm not too sure how I'll go about destroying the beasts.

I buy a quarter of a watermelon, enjoy a salad of melon, feta and mint for dinner (with broad beans on the side and strawberries for dessert), then whiz the remaining flesh in a blender, strain and pour into popsicle moulds for a future frozen treat. Then I leave the rind out before bed. Next day, I pop to the lottie before breakfast. I'm hugely disappointed not to find a single mollusc. If they did pay a visit, they happily moved on to digest in peace by daybreak. I think the boat-shaped rind might make an alluring receptacle for some beer, to lure them to a boozy grave, so I try that the next evening. Nope – not a single corpse to show for my efforts.

✳ summer herbs

After a couple of experimental years of growing herbs on the plot, I decided it's better to keep most summer herbs in pots at home, for proximity to the kitchen. I have a small concrete space outside my kitchen which is almost entirely occupied by a forest of herbs, and several more inside, especially basil, in pots on the kitchen windowsill.

Basil, parsley, mint, marjoram, oregano, dill, coriander, chives and tarragon are the summer stars. I rip them into salads, sauces, and soups every which way. At the moment it's broad beans and mint or marjoram, strawberries with basil, and everything in salad, but I'll soon be brandishing the soft and pungent leaves of all of the above with tomatoes, potatoes, courgettes and cucumbers too. There are few summer herb and vegetable or fruit combinations which are wrong, except possibly chives and fruit.

Opposite Floorboards rescued from a skip serve as temporary paths on the lottie.

Above A young cucumber plant ready to climb. **Right** Lettuces planted among onions and leeks, and as ever, weeds.

'Repotted or planted-out cucumbers will really be starting to take off now and will need some help with their skyward climb.'

support cucumbers

Repotted or planted-out cucumbers will really be starting to take off now and will need some help with their skyward climb. Long canes will suffice, though string is also effective, if you have something above the plants to tie it on to. Tie a string gently around the plant near the base of the stem. Wind it upwards around the stem, then tie to something sturdy well above the plant, but loosely so you can re-wind and re-tie as the plant grows.

sow chard and perpetual spinach

Chard is of great value in the garden – it's one of the easiest things to grow, has relatively few pests (although the slugs will have a go), it keeps coming back the more you cut it and it lasts nearly a year, right through winter. A 2m row is about right for a perpetual harvest if grown in the ground, but small quantities can be grown in a rectangular container. Swiss chard 'Bright Lights' is a gorgeous mixture of luminous ruby, yellow and orange-ribbed leaves, so it makes a beautiful display (see also page 32).

Sow up until August or as early as April. Sow thinly in a shallow drill directly in the ground and thin out when large enough to handle. I have been known to skip the thinning out step and still have a thriving crop, if a little crowded. The leaves can be harvested as babies for salad, then for cooking when larger. It's best to cut a few leaves from each plant rather than hacking off a great handful, though it will still come back even if you do this.

also Plant out celeriac seedlings 20cm–30cm apart.

Sow turnips directly in the soil.

grape leaves

I am fortunate to have access to two grapevines – one I inherited on the plot and one has extended from my Cypriot neighbour's into my home garden. If you don't have one, you may be able to forage some if you know what to look for. Just be sure that they won't have been sprayed. I had to retrain part of my allotment vine because it was growing on the fence facing the street, and the local Cypriot residents were stripping it before we had a chance!

The leaves have a citrussy tang and are tastiest and most tender in late spring and early summer. Roughly hand-sized leaves are perfect for stuffing – as for rice-stuffed dolmades. They can be soaked in boiling water first so they roll more easily. Otherwise, when young, treat them like any leafy green vegetable and wash and chop, then steam or fry. It is also possible to brine them for use throughout the year, something my Cypriot neighbour has explained to me but I have never done. I guess he makes a few more dolmades than I do!

late june
lloyd and suzanne

Lloyd and Suzanne have a magnificent and productive cherry tree on their plot. Alas, I do not, but they are extremely generous people, and supply me with cherries when the cornucopia overflows, as it is now. I repay them with any spare seedlings I might have going and broad beans. (I have tried to give some broad beans to Miss Gaynor, who, along with Fred, grows a large crop of 'red beans' or kidney beans for rice'n'peas, but she politely refused my offer, saying with a grimace, "In Jamaica we feed them to pigs." Fair enough.)

Suzanne leaves the plot with an enviable clutch of beetroot – already! Mine are a long way off. When I ask what plans she has for them, she ecstatically describes a recipe for a roasted beetroot and goat's cheese tart with dill and onions caramelised in wine and honey. I file that one away for my late summer beetroot harvest.

Lloyd and Suzanne are full of good ideas. Back in February, Dan and I pulled up to the plot in our van with heaps of twin-walled plastic sheeting that we found dumped in the woods, with the intention of building a greenhouse. This stuff costs a fortune to buy new, as would a new greenhouse, so we were hoping to achieve a triumph of thrift and recycling. I was extremely sceptical about this undertaking, but Dan is a master of construction and bodging, so I hoped he might be able to work a miracle. These plastic sheets were awkwardly large, riddled with moss and spider nests and not a pleasure to handle. We hosed them down and scrubbed them, then measured them up according to a diagram Dan had drawn. He got out the hacksaw and started cutting the first sheet while I braced it clumsily. In ten minutes, he had made an incision about a half a metre long. It was a bitterly cold afternoon and I was just about at the end of my tether – it was clear this project was just far too ambitious.

cherries

The best way to enjoy plump, sweet, juicy cherries during their short season is simply to gorge on them one by one, from bowl to mouth.

Cherries are particularly nice chilled. Also they are not half bad dipped in dark melted chocolate. Cherries and chocolate are a happy marriage, as in the seventies classic Black Forest Gateau. For a show-stopping dessert, try a Black Forest Pavlova: a large cocoa-flavoured meringue nest topped with a thick pillow of kirsch-spiked whipped cream, drizzled with dark chocolate ganache and topped with cherries, stone in and stem on.

Clafoutis, the French fruit tart in a Yorkshire pudding-style batter, is a classic cherry vehicle and you don't really need to pit them for that either. Pitting cherries for cooking is a tedious task, but a specially designed cherry pitter makes it a breeze if you need to get through a bushel. Pitted cherries can be frozen.

Opposite: clockwise from left Young broad beans dangling; newly formed recurrants; use a small knife to cut broad beans; tasty peashoots.

> **'It's a great shame, I know, but Midsummer Day (June 24) is traditionally the end of the asparagus season.'**

Then Lloyd came to the rescue. He approached and asked if we'd like to borrow his rechargeable circular saw, which he spoke of with great reverence as though it's one of his most prized possessions. I followed him home to collect it, and from that point on we were away. I'll never forget the horrendous noise of that saw grinding through those plastic sheets (and neither will the residents of the street lining the allotment site), but within about three hours, Dan had indeed worked magic, we had a 'new' greenhouse and a massive moveable coldframe to boot. I returned Lloyd's saw to him with a nice bottle of Rioja.

key jobs right now

stop harvesting asparagus
It's a great shame, I know, but Midsummer Day (June 24) is traditionally the end of the asparagus season. Oh yes, it will keep on coming and tempting you, but in order for the nutrients to be replenished for a healthy harvest next year, you must let it go. The silver lining is that you will be rewarded with a beautiful display of tall, feathery ferns with dangling green baubles. Once the ferns turn yellow in October, it's time to hack them down, leaving a small stump (see page 161).

plant out brassica seedlings
Seedlings that have reached 10–15cm will be ready to go into their final positions. They like firm ground, so dig the space over a bit first and them firm it down by compressing it underfoot. Allow more space than you might think for these mighty plants: about 1 square metre per plant. Birds, particularly pigeons, will have your seedlings for breakfast if you don't protect them, so cover the area with netting (see also page 44).

also Last chance to sow sweetcorn.

Last chance to sow or plant out runner bean plants.

Sow more lettuce.

Sow more brassicas for later winter and early spring crops.

Above Young sweetcorn should be planted out and under way now, but there's still just time to sow more.

 potatoes

Early and small maincrop potatoes should be ready now. This most versatile of veggies graces the table with abundance from now until the brink of winter. When digging up, slide the fork in gently so as not to spear them. Turn the soil over a few times and more magically appear, but dig up only the quantity you want to use. If processed from plot to plate within a few hours, they bring the same ambrosial pleasure as just-picked asparagus or sweetcorn – simply incomparable to shop-bought produce.

Small new potatoes are best scrubbed and boiled in salty water, perhaps with a sprig of mint. Eat whole or crush them while still hot and sprinkle with white wine vinegar and drizzle with olive oil. Once confronted with a glut later in the season, leave them on the soil surface and let them dry out before storing in a bag in a cool dry place. An apple or an orange in the bag deters rotting.

Rather than store potatoes, I prefer to go cook, crush, cool and then store in resealable plastic bags in the freezer.

broad bean + quinoa tabbouleh with apricots

Tabbouleh is traditionally made with bulghar wheat and a whole lot more parsley. This version capitalises on the nutritious wonder-grain, quinoa, which is high in protein and low-GI carbs, and has a wonderfully clean flavour.

200ml quinoa, measured by volume
400ml water
200g fresh young broad beans, shelled weight (frozen are also OK)
8 dried apricots, coarsely chopped

Grated zest of 1 large lemon
3 tbsp fresh lemon juice
3 tbsp extra virgin olive oil
Sea salt and freshly ground black pepper

4 spring onions, chopped
4 tbsp fresh chopped mint
4 tbsp fresh chopped parsley
1 large vine tomato, chopped (optional)

Heat a lidded saucepan over a moderate flame. Add the quinoa to the dry pan and shake until the grain is lightly toasted and popping. Add the water, stir and bring to the boil, then reduce the heat to a simmer. Cover and cook for 10 minutes, then add the broad beans and apricots and stir once. Keep covered and cook for a further 3–5 minutes, or just until the water is absorbed but the grains are still separate, the beans are steamed to tenderness and the apricots plumped. Remove from the pan, spread out on a tray and allow to cool completely.

Mix together the lemon zest and juice, olive oil and salt and pepper. When the quinoa is cool, combine in a bowl with the dressing and the chopped onion, herbs, and tomato, if using. **Serves 4**

Prep tip More mature broad beans have toughened skins, but go ahead and use them anyway and don't bother to peel – the skins are a good bit of fibre for the system!

parmesan potato cakes with summer herbs

Use whatever summer herbs are available, but give mint a miss as it will clash with the Parmesan. Don't fry these cakes as they will fall apart – brown them nicely in the dry pan like bubble and squeak.

750g potatoes, peeled and cut in large chunks
Sea salt

1 tsp white wine vinegar
75g Parmesan, finely grated
Freshly ground black pepper
2 tbsp capers in vinegar, drained
Large handful of parsley, chopped

Large handful of basil, chopped
1 sprig oregano or marjoram, stripped and roughly chopped
1 sprig tarragon, stripped and roughly chopped
A few chives, chopped
Virgin rapeseed or sunflower oil

Place the potatoes in a pan and cover with boiling water. Add salt and bring to the boil. Cook until the potatoes are soft, about 15 minutes. Drain and leave in the colander for a couple of minutes, then place in a bowl. Sprinkle with the vinegar, add the Parmesan and grind in plenty of pepper. Use a fork to blend and crush the potatoes, leaving the texture a little lumpy instead of making a totally smooth puree. Leave to cool.

Stir the capers and herbs through the potato mixture. Rub a little oil on your hands, then form the mixture into 10–12 flat-ish cakes. Cook now or chill the cakes on a plate until ready to cook.

Smear a tiny bit of oil in a large non-stick pan and place over a medium heat. Place the cakes in the pan and cook on each side, without pushing around, until crisp and golden, about 5–7 minutes each side. Serve hot.
Serves 4

artichoke carpaccio

A yummy salad of young raw artichokes.

Prepare a few small artichokes: cut the top off, pare away all the tough parts around the heart to leave the pale core, cut in half top to bottom and scrape out the hairs with a teaspoon. Leave in a bowl of lemony water while you prepare the rest. Slice each one as thinly as possible and coat in lemon juice, then serve on small plates with salt, olive oil, Parmesan shavings and a few baby garden leaves.

the ultimate artichoke

...and how to eat it. In my opinion, this is the best way to tackle and serve artichokes in all their glory, with a simple lemon pepper mayo sauce. This would be my last supper, if I had to choose. See also the microwave method at the bottom, if you are in a hurry – it's not quite as good as boiling them, but much quicker.

Artichokes
Water
Salt
White wine vinegar or cider
  vinegar
Oil

For the dipping sauce
4 tbsp mayonnaise
Juice of ½ lemon
Freshly ground black pepper

Bring a large pan of water to the boil and season it with a generous dose of salt and a good glug of vinegar for flavour, plus a drop of oil which gives the artichokes a slight gloss.

Slice the stem off the artichoke(s), flush to the base. If very spikey snip off the tips of the leaves or slice about a quarter clean off the top. Boil the artichoke(s) until a leaf pulled away from half way to the centre comes away easily, about 20–40 minutes, depending on the size and quantity. Remove from the water with a slotted spoon and drain upside down on a towel.

Make the dressing in a small bowl. Beat the mayonnaise with the fresh lemon juice, grind tons of black pepper into it and stir.

Dip the plump end of each leaf in the dressing, pulling off all the sweet flesh with your teeth. Once you get to the hairy centre (the choke), use a small knife to shave off just the hairs, working around the edge with a sawing motion, leaving the succulent base. This is the best bit – your reward. Savour every delectable mouthful with the lemon dressing.

Microwave method: Drain the soaked artichoke(s) (see prep tip below) and place in a microwaveable container with a couple of tablespoons of water and cover. One 300g choke should take about 8–9 minutes on high power; stand covered for 5 minutes. Taste for doneness and give it a few more minutes if it's still tough.

Prep tip To de-bug, first soak the artichokes in a bowl of cold water with a couple of tablespoons of vinegar added.

JULY	INDOORS OR UNDER GLASS	OUTDOORS DIRECT IN SO
Beetroot		
Broad beans		
Broccoli (calabrese)		
Broccoli (sprouting)		
Cabbage (summer)		
Cabbage (spring)	★	★
Carrots		
Cauliflower		
Chard		★
Cherries		
Courgettes/summer squashes		
Cucumbers		
Fennel		
Flowers (edible/companion)		
Garlic		
Globe artichokes		
Kale		
Lettuce/salad leaves	★	★
Onions/shallots		
Pea shoots	★	★
Peas		
Perpetual spinach	★	★
Potatoes		
Radishes	★	★
Rhubarb		
Rocket	★	★
Runner beans/other beans		
Spinach	★	★
Spring onions	★	★
Strawberries		★
Summer berries		
Summer herbs	★	★
Swedes		★
Tomatoes		
Turnips		★
Winter herbs	★	★

UITABLE FOR CONTAINERS	HARVESTING NOW	RECIPES AND OTHER INFORMATION
★	★	*see 138*
★	★	broad bean tabbouleh, 92; *see also 68, 75, 112*
★	★	*see 98*
★	★	psb + barley risotto, 39; *see also 35*
★	★	lemony lentil cabbage parcels, 203; *see also 123*
★		hot + sour swede + cabbage salad, 200
★	★	*see 167, 179*
★	★	cauliflower + coconut soup, 182; *see 172, 183*
★	★	sorrel + chard kuku, 36; *see also 32, 39, 57*
★	★	*see 89*
★	★	warm courgette salad, 113; *see also 102, 128, 148*
★	★	smoky gazpacho, 128; *see also 105, 167*
★	★	*see 140*
★	★	*see 116*
★	★	broad bean + garlic purée; *see also 39, 55, 75, 100*
	★	ultimate artichoke, 94; *see also 80, 93,*
★	★	saffron rice broth + winter greens, 38; *see also 42*
★	★	broad beans with lettuce, 75; *see also 57, 63*
★	★	*see 36, 39, 75, 161*
★	★	*see 67*
★	★	pea + feta egg cups, 72; *see also 67*
★	★	*see 32*
★	★	parmesan potato cakes, 93; *see also 57, 91*
★	★	*see 64*
	★	rhubarb + lentil curry, 75; *see also 52, 56*
★	★	green soup, 57; *see 46*
★	★	soy glazed runner beans, 112; *see also 106, 127, 131*
★	★	*see 32*
★	★	green soup, 57; *see also 61, 72, 92, 112, 131*
★	★	*see 83*
★	★	*see 108*
★	★	parmesan potato cakes, 93; *see also 28, 84*
★		hot + sour swede + cabbage salad, 200; *see also 197*
★	★	sweetcorn + spiced avocado soup, 131; *see also 119*
★	★	*see 180*
★	★	*see 150, 169, 198*

early july
here come the courgettes...

✳ summer broccoli

It's worth planting quick-growing summer broccoli in March to enjoy now. Calabrese is the type that you will know as ordinary broccoli, as opposed to the sprouting types of late winter and spring. The plants produce a large head followed by smaller sprouts once the main head is cut. Think of it as a giant cluster of flower buds – you want to catch it just as the tiny buds are fully formed but before they burst into flower.

Compare the cut broccoli head to a tree: the stem, or 'trunk' is one of the most delicious parts, so don't waste it. Shave off the 'bark' with a sharp knife – the outermost green casing is too tough to eat, but the pale green core of the stem is sweet.

Broccoli is a superfood with anti-carcinogenic properties and a host of valuable vitamins and minerals, so cook it with care. Steaming is best. Cooking in the microwave is acceptable, add just a sprinkle of water or you'll lose nutrients as they leach into the water. Don't overcook it or it goes tough

As the emergence of the first asparagus spear spells the arrival of spring, the first courgette confirms that it is now truly summer. Every crop has its firsts; these are thrilling moments, especially when you take the first bite. Since I've become an urban farmer, my sense of seasonality has become much more acute. I don't buy courgettes in winter anymore, or ever for that matter. I enjoy them from the garden only during their short and prolific season, from now until summer makes its exit in late September.

The first cucumber has also appeared, so this signals what always becomes a tidal wave of curcubits. As with courgettes, the cucumbers taste at their absolute best when harvested small. Types vary, but for both, I try to cut them when they have a girth of a peeled banana. There are always a few that get overlooked and turn into monstrous club-size specimens seemingly overnight. The leafier the plants become, the more difficult it is to spot them, but then it's time to eat the leaves...

I kid you not. Discovering the culinary merits of squash leaves was one of my all-time highlights of allotment life, and continues to be so. This came about a couple of years ago when a man drove up to the lottie in late August. As I was inspecting my squashes, he got out of his car, breathless, and said, with a heavy accent, "I've been coming past for days hoping to find someone here!" I thought maybe he'd lost his pet or something. "Please," he begged, "can I have some of your flowers?" "Which ones?" I asked. "Those," he said, pointing to the squashes. "Oh yes," I said, "they are good!" "And please," he said, "the leaves as well, and stems."

Opposite: clockwise from top left A ripe 'Burpless Tasty Green' cucumber: if prickly rub with a sponge when washing; delicious yellow courgettes and blossoms, set to dominate the menu for a few weeks; baby courgettes are especially tasty as are the blossoms; cucumber plants are happy in recycled woven plastic potato bags.

I'd never tried the leaves, so I asked him what he does with them. "Just chop them," he replied, "fry onion in oil, add the leaves and water – that's it. Soup! Or," he continued, "just fry with garlic and add dried chilli. The flowers – you can stuff them with meat and steam them, or make tempura. That's the best way." He also advised me that my green tomatoes would make a good pickle, salted and packed in oil with mustard seeds and chilli.

I filled a bag with smallish pumpkin and courgette leaves (he assured me they lose their prickles in the cooking) and a few flowers, some with courgettes attached. He offered money but of course I refused. He's from Mauritius. He pointed to his house, which faces the allotment, and said he's rather immobile and doesn't get out much. I told him I'd drop off some more at his doorstep in a few days, which I did, and he's been back to visit a few times.

So, we've been feasting on pumpkin and courgette leaves ever since, whenever the plants get unruly and throw out tender young shoots. I try not to decimate the plant obviously, so it's a fortnightly treat from mid-July onwards. The prickles do subside in the cooking, but you are left with a wonderful, lightly abrasive 'mouth-feel' (a term I don't like but that's the best way to describe it), and an inimitable big, sweet, earthy flavour (see also page 124).

✳ wet garlic

Now's the time to enjoy that over-wintering garlic which has been so long in coming. The top growth will have gone brown and may have flopped over by now, so it's time to dig it up. Fresh from the ground, it is known as wet garlic.

At this stage the flavour is mild and you can eat the whole bulb, skins and all, before they dry out completely. Simply remove the dry parts, slice the bulb and chop into cooking, crush into salad dressing or blend into pesto. Or leave the bulbs and dead growth intact, tie together and hang to dry.

key jobs right now

get more out of your strawberries

If you haven't already, it's not too late to start a strawberry bed for next year, so buy in some plants. On an allotment, you may find that one of your neighbours has plants to give away. Established strawberry plants will be throwing out runners now, which will naturally proliferate in the bed if left to their own devices. For a border-controlled space and healthier plants, remove these runners.

Opposite Remove strawberry runners for healthier plants.

If you are happy to have more strawberries but want to contain the plants, you can train the runners to a convenient location and peg them down with a thick staple in 3 or 4 places to encourage them to take root. You can even put pots of compost under the runners and peg them in. Once they've rooted in the pot, snip the runner to separate them and move them elsewhere or give them away. Strawberries are also ideal for growing in containers.

keep sowing The sowing season will be all but over by the end of this month. You can still sow some winter brassicas, which you will be able to plant in patches where other crops have finished later, like peas, broad beans, potatoes, etc. Keep sowing quick crops like lettuce and radishes. More carrots, beetroot, chard and even a final pea crop can still be sown until the end of the month.

'Established strawberry plants will be throwing out runners now, which will naturally proliferate in the bed if left to their own devices.'

mid-july
scaling the peak

The lottie is such an exciting place to be at the moment, with everything peaking abundantly. It's a lush and vibrant vegetable paradise exploding in a climax of produce. In two or three more weeks I expect to get the feeling that we are over the hump and beginning the season's descent. But for now, it's high-summer heaven.

Allotment duty in July is a never-ending chain of necessary jobs, but it has to be put in its place – I can't let it take over my life completely. It's currently reserved for balmy, bright evenings, ideally interspersed with sips from a frosty glass of rosé, which sits twinkling in the low sunlight on the potting table. However, July can be a temperamental month in the UK. In recent years, July has been a complete washout. There's plenty to get on with, but rainy gardening is about as much fun as a rainy picnic. For one thing, the plot is a lonely place; no cats, no fellow allotmenteers braving the showers, no children laughing in the street, not even the birds want any of it. Muddy soil gets compressed underfoot which is not good and, with only slugs and snails for company, I've come to the conclusion that it's not even worth a visit in the rain.

One year around this time, I watched in horror from my home office window as, for ten long minutes, gallons of hailstones shredded my pansies and de-petalled my geraniums. It stopped abruptly and I dashed to the plot, wading through freakish drifts of ice gravel, terrified of what I'd find. It was as if someone had taken a machine gun to my beloved plants. The squash leaves were full of holes and some swelling pumpkins pockmarked, the runner beans were in tatters, and infant tomatoes had been sliced clean off the plants. Everything suffered war wounds and I was devastated, but a couple of weeks later it had all bounced back with astonishing resilience.

courgettes and squashes

This is a productive time for courgettes and other thin-skinned squash varieties like crookneck, patty pan and gem. From three plants, I am cutting 4 or 5 courgettes a day in mid-July, though some inevitably get overlooked and turn into marrows. Cut as soon as you discover them so the plant redirects its energy to producing more fruit. Take care when picking them as some have turgid, prickly hairs which can stick in the skin.

Courgettes are at their sweetest when small; enhance their flavour by judicious cooking and seasoning. I have a two-sided non-stick contact grill, which has never seen a piece of meat but is perfect for grilling courgettes, either small ones halved lengthways, or thick slices of larger ones. I cook them, lightly coated in oil or sometimes without, until they are juicy and branded with grill marks, but still a little firm. I sprinkle them with a little wine vinegar, salt and pepper while still hot and eat either warm or cold with chopped mint.

'In recent years, July has been a complete washout. There's plenty to get on with, but rainy gardening is about as much fun as a rainy picnic.'

Above left Rain is great for the garden but not the best time for gardening.
Above right A giant sunflower, so heavy it's bowing like a showerhead, harvested fennel in hand.

A few weeks ago, a couple of mystery squashes appeared in the brassica patch, and I was so curious as to what they might turn out to be I let them stay. Now they are surpassing most of the purpose-planted ones, with gargantuan leaves and twenty-foot long tendrils that are visibly growing about a foot a day – they are positively dominating the plot. So far no fruits are developing on them, but I'm happy to keep them even just for the edible leaves and the impressive display. But like with a gaggle of unruly school kids, I have to discipline them daily to stop them running into the street.

key jobs right now

Below Potted mint gets root-bound and needs dividing every couple of years.

control herbs
The more you cut and use your summer and winter herbs, the more they will thrive. By now they are almost certainly at the flowering stage (or beyond it depending on planting time and the weather). Keep pinching out the tips and the flowers to encourage fuller growth and to stop the plants getting leggy, especially soft summer herbs like mint, basil and tarragon. Eat the pinchings, naturally! Leave some of your dill, mint and coriander to flower and then go to seed (see page 84), and you can always sow more.

Mint is really best grown in containers as it can be invasive in the ground. The mint's roots will quickly fill its container, so it's a good idea to divide the plant in two and replant in fresh compost every couple of years.

Woody, perennial winter herbs like rosemary and thyme can be pruned of their wily shoots and trimmed to shape when the flowering subsides.

sow swedes and turnips
It's time to consider getting some of these winter vegetables underway. Swedes in particular are a much-maligned vegetable, but they do have their place on

the table if treated properly (see page 197). These veg are cheap to buy, but when so many other crops have gone by the wayside in winter, it's nice to have a few more things to look forward to in the cold months, and they both taste so much better fresh from the ground than store-bought.

Swedes and turnips are both in the brassica family, so they should be grown in a place where brassicas were not grown the previous year, so not with the other root veg. Both are simple to grow and can be sown directly in shallow drills, then thinned out once the shoots are large enough to handle, as you would beetroot, giving them up to 15cm to swell.

also If runner beans have reached beyond their supports, nip off the tops to encourage more beans in the reachable areas.

With cordon tomatoes, cut off the leaf tips from the main stem above the fourth truss to encourage fruits to ripen. This will encourage more side shoots, so keep nipping them off. Bush varieties can be left to do their thing.

If you have any lettuces which have bolted, they will be too bitter to eat. Be ruthless – yank them up and compost them – they'll just be sucking nutrition out of the soil.

cucumbers

Like their courgette sisters, cucumbers often seem to appear out of the blue and should be cut small for the best flavour. Larger ones develop more seeds but are still delicious.

Like courgettes, they too keep well in the fridge for well over a week. Their life can be extended by simple pickling – slice thinly and sprinkle with salt, layering them up in a colander over the sink and leave to drain for a couple of hours. Place them in a bowl and stir a little sugar through them, then cover with rice vinegar or wine vinegar. Nibble them out of the fridge and as each day passes they get tastier.

I also like to make a refreshing cold soup with cucumbers – chop and puree them with yoghurt, mint, lemon, crushed garlic and salt, and a couple of handfuls of walnuts.

late july
ulrika

When we were first granted our plot in 2005, we couldn't believe our luck. After a three-and-a-half-year wait, we got the letter through the postbox telling us our number was up and asking did we still want a plot. After responding with a resounding "YES," I was met by the man from the council who unlocked the site for me for the first time. Examining a diagram, he showed me the location and dimensions of Plot No 5.

I couldn't believe the size of it. Plot No 5 was one of only two disused plots on the eight-plot site, and it was the biggest of them all! I had to get him to reconfirm it a few times over and show me the boundaries – all the way from the shed to the skip. Yes, this 100-ish metre square wilderness of nettles and brambles was ours for the cultivating.

Ulrika in Plot No 8 had been there a few years before we arrived on the scene. It was refreshing to see that someone my age or younger and female was using a plot, and that it wasn't just the preserve of old men anymore. I've always felt a little guilty though, because Ulrika's plot is a small strip in the back corner of the site surrounded by trees, which suck the nutrition out of her soil and limit the light. Nonetheless she grows a staggeringly beautiful array of edible and ornamental flowers and herbs like lemon verbena and liquorice, wild salad leaves like mizuna, and dozens of plants from her native Sweden that are thus far untranslated. In the face of less than ideal conditions, she has created her own delicious little corner of paradise in North London, which is at its most exuberant in late July.

✳ runner beans

Runners, French beans, or whatever climbing or dwarf variety you might be growing can be enjoyed at all stages for the rest of summer – especially when young, eaten pod and all. There are just too many varieties to mention, so I'll focus on runner beans.

They're best if you can catch the pods before they reach the stringy stage, anything up to 15–20cm long, but this is nigh on impossible once the runner bean tsunami gathers momentum. In my experience, larger ones are usually stringy, even the 'stringless' varieties.

Runner beans are pretty much past it once the seeds in the pod are visible, having reached the diameter of small peas and they go 'pop' when you squeeze them through the pod. They are still edible, but you'll need to remove the strings from the edges of the pods by shaving them off with a potato peeler or sharp knife.

Runner beans in the pod and in their prime are best sliced and steamed, or blanched to preserve the colour, bagged up and frozen in portions (see also page 127

Opposite Late July is paradise on the plot.

✳ summer berries

Gooseberries may be past it now, but raspberries and currants of all colours will be ready for picking. Hedgerow blackberries will be starting to ripen. These nutritious berries are wonderful cooked in pies and tarts or summer pudding.

Blackcurrants are awesome fruits with a dazzling flavour and a strong dye in the juice. Snip off the trusses with scissors when picking. This is a tedious business but you won't need to de-stem or de-seed them, just chuck them in the pan with some sugar and strain later. I usually make a compote, strain it, cool it and freeze it – instant sorbet! Or thaw and use it stirred into yoghurt or drinks.

Red and white currants make a glamorous garnish for desserts, but are quite sharp and preferable for cooking or jam making. Just rinse and freeze them if you don't have time to use the harvest right away. Freeze on a tray first, then bag up if you want to use small quantities at a time. The same goes for blackberries. Raspberries are hard to beat just eaten raw.

cut down spent broad beans These should be winding up by now if not completely finished (your over-wintering crop certainly will be). As with all members of the legume family, broad beans fix nitrogen in the soil through their roots, so rather than pulling up the plants, hack them down at the base and leave the roots in the soil. The stems can go in the compost bin.

Soon, or even now, this space will be a good place to plant some more winter brassica seedlings which you may have coming up from June sowings (it's still not too late to sow some more in pots if not). Brassicas are slow-growing, hungry feeders and will happily grow in this bean-nourished area. Just remember to keep track (I use a calendar hanging in the shed) of what you are growing where and when so that you don't repeat crops in the same space next year. In other words, if you do grow some long-term brassicas here, you'll need to follow on next year with roots or tomatoes or something other than legumes (or brassicas).

stay on disease patrol Drought or extreme heat can put stress on plants, making them more susceptible to diseases and pests which might be lurking around the corner. Ideally you will have already armed yourself with a good disease recognition manual. *The Vegetable and Herb Expert* by Dr D.G. Hessayon is my bible, and though he is a bit heavy-handed with the chemical warfare, it's a good diagnostic, for spotting unusual developments on the plants, identifying the problem and dealing with it before it destroys a crop.

Potato blight, which also affects tomatoes, usually strikes in mid to late summer, especially if it has been a soggy one. The first sign is brown blotches on the edges of the leaves of both plants. Once the disease has taken hold, it is impossible to eradicate and might return for years to come.

If you spot it on potato foliage (once you are sure that is the correct diagnosis – check a manual or ask your neighbours), lop off the foliage and destroy it – don't compost. Leave the potatoes in the ground for about two weeks before digging up as needed. If the potatoes themselves look or smell funny then it might have been too late.

If you've spotted blight on your tomatoes, there may be no hope for them. One preventative measure early on is to water the plants only at the roots rather than letting the leaves get wet. Not to sound too negative, but speaking as the sad loser of a whole crop to blight one grim summer, if it's a rainy month to come, the tomatoes could still be doomed. However, if this does happen, most of the unaffected green tomatoes can still be ripened on the windowsill at home or cooked and eaten, so all is not lost.

also Keep feeding your tomatoes and aubergines.

'Broad beans fix nitrogen in the soil through their roots, so rather than pulling up the plants, hack them down at the base and leave the roots in the soil.'

Above Broad beans will be nearing their end now.

warm courgette salad with parmesan crackling

The courgette slices here get fried in the fat released by the Parmesan, which then turns into a 'sinful' crusty crackling in the pan, clinging to the lightly cooked courgettes. Served on a bed of garden leaves and walnuts, it makes a substantial main-course salad for 2, especially with the addition of a few boiled new potatoes. Otherwise the recipe will serve 4 as an accompaniment.

350g courgettes (about 2 medium), sliced into 3/4cm thick discs
1½ tbsp best balsamic vinegar
Mixed salad leaves
50g walnuts, broken into smallish pieces
75g best Parmesan, finely grated
2 tbsp extra virgin olive oil
Pinch of sea salt
Freshly ground black pepper

Heat your largest non-stick frying pan over a low to medium heat. Place the courgette discs in a bowl and sprinkle with the balsamic vinegar. Turn to coat.

Prepare serving plates with salad leaves and sprinkle with walnuts.

Place the courgettes in the hot, dry pan (save the remaining vinegar left in the bowl). Do not crowd the pan – leave some space between the courgette slices. Do it in two batches if your pan isn't large enough. Sprinkle half the grated Parmesan over the courgettes, letting some fall to the bottom of the pan. You want a crusty filigree of Parmesan to crisp up on the bottom of the pan, so do not stir. When the cheese starts to melt and release its fat, watch carefully. When the cheese starts to look golden and crusty, turn over the courgettes and scrape the cheese from the pan – they will stick together and that's fine – the cheese may stick to your spatula, so use a knife to scrape it off back into the pan. Sprinkle the remaining cheese over the turned courgettes and let it get crusty again, without burning. Turn once more, then remove the pan from the heat.

Beat the olive oil into the remaining vinegar in the bowl with a pinch of salt. Divide the courgettes amongst the salad plates, drizzle with the dressing and grind over plenty of black pepper. **Serves 2 as a main course or 4 as an accompaniment**

Prep tip You could use part of an overgrown courgette for this. If the skin seems too tough, remove it, scrape out the seeds if large and slice into 3/4cm thick half-moons. Baby courgettes can also be used, sliced lengthwise as above left.

soy-glazed runner beans with whole egg + cashews

There is usually a glut of runner beans during their peak season, and this utilises rather a lot of them for a satisfying spicy dinner for two. Choose young pods without visible beans inside, otherwise you will have to remove the strings with a paring knife. The eggs here are boiled for a short time so that the yolks are semi-cooked and buttery.

2 organic eggs

6 medium cloves garlic
1cm piece ginger, peeled and finely grated
Pinch of coarse sea salt
2 spring onions, roughly chopped
1 red chilli, roughly chopped

2 tbsp sunflower oil + a little more
50g raw cashews
500g runner beans, cut in small segments
1 tbsp dark soy sauce
1 tbsp rice vinegar or cider vinegar
1 tbsp dark brown sugar

Boiled plain rice or egg noodles, to serve

Place the eggs in a pan of cold water and bring to the boil. After 5 minutes, drain, rinse and let the eggs stand in cold water until cool, then peel.

In a mortar, pound the garlic and ginger with a pinch of coarse salt until a paste results. Add the spring onions and chilli and pound a bit more. Set aside. (Alternatively, crush the garlic in another fashion and mix with the other ingredients.)

Heat a wok until very hot, then add 2 tbsp oil. Add cashew nuts and fry briefly until golden. Remove with a slotted spoon and drain on kitchen paper.

To the hot oil, add the runner beans. Stir-fry briskly for about 13–15 minutes, until very soft and slightly charred. Add a dash more oil, then the garlic mixture. Fry briefly until fragrant, then add the soy sauce and vinegar and crumble in the sugar. Stir until evenly combined. Add the peeled eggs. Stir gently and coat with the sauce. Take the wok off the heat.

Serve the beans with one egg per person on a bed of rice. Top with fried cashews. **Serves 2**

broad bean + roasted garlic puree

A luxury broad bean hummous, if you will. Even mature, thick-skinned beans can be used – the skins might not blend in completely, but add a nice chewy texture. Serve with fresh crunchy crudités.

1 large or 2 small bulbs garlic, wet or dried

300g broad beans (shelled weight – frozen can be used)

4 tbsp extra virgin olive oil + more to drizzle

Finely grated zest of 1 lemon
2 tbsp fresh lemon juice
6 fresh basil tips or about 16 leaves
Large pinch of sea salt
Freshly ground black pepper

Preheat the oven to 180°C (350°F). Cut the prepared garlic in half equatorially – that is, through the middle of each clove rather than top to bottom. Coat lightly in oil and place in a small roasting dish, cut side up. Roast until golden, anywhere from 20–40 minutes depending on the size. Leave until cool enough to handle, then squeeze the roasted flesh out of the papery skins into a small bowl.

Steam the broad beans for 3–5 minutes, until tender. While still hot, place the beans in a food processor. Add the roasted garlic, about 8 tbsp of the steaming water, and the remaining ingredients. Process on high for a good few minutes, until as smooth as possible. Taste for seasoning and adjust both the flavour and texture if necessary, adding a little more cooking liquid if you feel it's too stiff, and perhaps a tad more lemon juice or salt.

Scoop the puree into a bowl, drizzle with a little more olive oil and grind black pepper over it. Serve with crunchy raw vegetables. It's also nice cold and can be stored covered in the fridge for up to three days. **Serves 4–6**

Prep tip Peel just the outer layer of the garlic to keep the bulb intact, trim the frilly end by snapping or slicing it off, and wash away any remaining mud.

courgette jerky

Shrunken courgettes – perfect for using up a glut and especially overgrown ones.

Heat the oven to 150°C (300°F). If the courgettes are mature and have large seeds, remove them. Slice into very thin pieces – rectangles or discs – place in a bowl, add a tiny bit of salt and dribble oil over them, then use hands to coat each slice. Lay on parchment-lined baking sheets and cook until shrunken, dry but pliable, and golden, about 45 minutes. Eat as a snack or add to salads.

roasted courgette soup

A superlative soup.

Cover the bottom of a roasting pan with chunks of courgette and several whole cloves of garlic. Coat in olive oil and add a few drops of good vinegar and seasoning. Roast in a 200°C (400°F) oven until browned and shrunken. Scrape the contents into a saucepan, barely cover with boiling water, then puree, leaving a little texture. Adjust seasoning. Serve hot or cold.

AUGUST	SOW INDOORS/UNDER GLASS	SOW OUTDOORS/IN SOIL
Aubergines		
Beetroot		
Broad beans		
Broccoli (calabrese)		
Cabbage (spring)	★	★
Cabbage (summer)		
Carrots		
Cauliflower		
Chard	★	★
Cherries		
Courgettes/summer squashes		
Cucumbers		
Fennel		
Flowers (edible/companion)		
Globe artichokes		
Kale		
Lettuce/salad leaves	★	★
Onions/shallots		
Oriental greens	★	★
Pea shoots		
Peas		
Peppers and chillies		
Perpetual spinach	★	★
Plums		
Potatoes		
Radishes	★	★
Rocket	★	★
Runner beans/other beans		
Spinach	★	★
Spring onions	★	★
Strawberries		
Summer berries		
Summer herbs		
Sweetcorn		
Tomatoes		
Turnips		★
Winter herbs	★	★

UITABLE FOR CONTAINERS	HARVESTING NOW	RECIPES AND OTHER INFORMATION
★	★	thai smoked aubergine salad, 167; *see also 124, 155*
★	★	*see 138*
★	★	broad bean tabbouleh, 92; *see also 68, 75, 112*
★	★	*see 98*
★	★	hot + sour swede + cabbage salad, 200
★	★	lemony lentil cabbage parcels, 203; *see also 123*
★	★	*see 167, 179*
★	★	cauliflower + coconut soup, 182; *see 172, 183*
★	★	sorrel + chard kuku, 36; *see also 32, 39, 57*
★	★	*see 89*
★	★	warm courgette salad, 113; *see also 102, 128, 148*
★	★	smoky gazpacho, 128; *see also 105, 167*
★	★	*see 140*
★	★	*see 116*
	★	ultimate artichoke, 94; *see also 80, 93,*
★	★	saffron rice broth + winter greens, 38; *see also 42*
★	★	broad beans with lettuce, 75; *see also 57, 63*
★	★	*see 36, 39, 75, 161*
★		*see 181*
★	★	*see 6/*
★	★	pea + feta egg cups, 72; *see also 67*
★	★	*see 112, 131, 143, 144*
★	★	*see 32*
★	★	*see 137*
★	★	parmesan potato cakes, 93; *see also 57, 91*
★	★	*see 64*
★	★	green soup, 57; *see 46*
★	★	soy glazed runner beans, 112; *see also 106, 127, 131*
★	★	*see 32*
★	★	green soup, 57; *see also 61, 72, 92, 112, 131*
★	★	*see 83*
★	★	*see 108*
★	★	parmesan potato cakes, 93; *see also 28, 84*
★	★	sweetcorn + spiced avocado soup, 131; *see also 119*
★	★	slow-roasted tomatoes, 131; *see also 120, 158, 166*
★	★	*see 180*
★	★	*see 150, 169, 198*

early august
life is... as I sowed it

✳ **nasturtiums**

Beautiful nasturtiums will have been sporting their neon orange or yellow blooms for several weeks now, faithfully deterring pest insects, attracting pollinators and adding welcome colour contrast to the verdant plotscape. You may even have had to discipline them already by cutting back, as they tend to get a little over-successful in the height of the season.

Cuttings of leaf, stem and flower can, of course, be composted, but don't forget, both are also delicious in salads, with a distinctive sweet peppery flavour like strong watercress – so strong it can make your eyes water!

Choose smaller leaves, as large ones have a slight (though not unpleasant) viscosity to them. To prepare the flowers, snip off the end of the funnel-shaped tail of the flower and rinse through with a gentle stream of water, which should clear out any insects that might be hiding.

This is the time of year when, I have to admit, I start to feel a little overwhelmed with vegetables. I've invested months of nurturing and now it's reap, reap, reap the rewards. I return from the plot each evening laden with bags of runner beans, courgettes, spring onions, calabrese, lettuce, rocket and potatoes. By the time everything is sorted, scrubbed, debugged and deslugged, chopped, cooked and seasoned or freezer-ready, I've practically lost the will to eat. It's all very well growing your own and eating it, but what rarely gets a mention is the toil of preparing it all for the pan or the plate. I live to cook and eat, and I'm the captain of the ship in the kitchen, so although Dan's a great help, it sometimes feels like I'm on a one-woman sailboat with a weighty vegetal cargo lost at sea.

It's funny how Dan and I automatically assume roles down on the plot and back in the kitchen. Somehow by default, he takes charge of most of the watering, pest control, skip-raiding and creative construction; while I'm the mistress of sowing, planting out, harvesting, preparing and cooking. One of Dan's triumphs is making the shed so cosy, it's practically a second home. We can take refuge from the rain in there with our two camping chairs and a desk, lamp, minor sound system, and a mini-fridge that he rigged up to run off a car battery he rescued from the street. We have been known to hang out there until well after dark. Our allotment contract states that we have a curfew of 10pm.

Another rule set out by the council is that we mustn't sell our produce. That's fine by me, though as a veritable vegetable factory at the moment, I could be making a killing. We give away quite a lot to the vicar and his wife who live opposite, to friends and to inquisitive passers-by, and we arrive at the odd dinner party bearing veg instead of the usual bottle of wine. Ulrika isn't able to grow

Left Twigs are always useful around the plot for holding up netting and staking plants. **Above** Plastic carrier bags are reused for the gathering the harvest of perpetual greens and herbs and also lining the home compost container.

certain things in her shady corner, so I offload some of the surplus on her, whereupon she reciprocates with her herbal home-grown tisanes, berries and flowers.

One crop, however, I hoard selfishly, and that's sweetcorn. Each plant only produces one or two ears, and as they become ready, it's a sweetcorn-munching lovefest back at our household. The first two ripe ears came off the plants this week and within minutes we were devouring the sugary pearls. Four months of nurturing – gone in 60 seconds of crisp, juicy bliss.

'One of Dan's triumphs is making the shed so cosy, it's practically a second home.'

check brassicas for pests

Bold as they are, brassicas are highly susceptible to pests of all kinds and, at this time of year, caterpillars and tiny white butterflies will be closing in. Check under the leaves near the stem. Blast them off with a stream of water or spray with a weak soap solution and then blast them. Or you may have to resort to a safe chemical spray. Look out also for a thick white fungus which distorts the leaves – take off the affected bits and throw them away. As I said last month, arm yourself with a manual for pest and disease identification to catch them early and take action (see page 108). But don't get too obsessive. Take it in your stride – it's all part of growing your own.

turn compost

At this stage of the game, there has probably been an increase in the amount of vegetable matter that's gone into the compost bin in the form of bean pods and other harvest remnants. Rising temperatures will be breaking the compost down, but now is a good time to help it along a little by turning it. This should really be done about every six to eight weeks, but especially now.

A stir or poke around with a hoe or fork from time to time is a good idea, but turning is easy if you have a purpose-built slightly conical compost bin. Just lift the bin to release the pile. Put the bin in its new position, ideally next to the old spot, then shovel the compost back into it. Some of the matter at the bottom may be ready to use, so if it looks and smells earthy, rich and crumbly, scatter that around plants for a boost and let the worms work their magic.

You can also improve the texture of the compost by incorporating some fibrous material into it as you shovel it back into the bin. Grass cuttings are perfect. You might try asking for some at a school or golf course – a dog-free environment is best, so not the park. Don't add a whole bag of grass cuttings all at once, but layer it in to the compost.

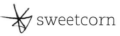 sweetcorn

In France some regard sweetcorn as fit only for cattle feed. Well, they don't know what they're missing. Ears of perfectly ripe sweetcorn, taken from plot to plate in 10 minutes flat, is another summer highlight.

Judging ripeness is tricky. The ear should be a good size, and sport a chocolate-brown hairdo with its dangling tassel, which is soft and silky, not dry and brittle. Pull back part of the sheath to reveal the kernels. At the top, the kernels are smaller and paler, so it's difficult to judge by size or colour. Squeeze a kernel with a fingernail: if it squirts out a watery liquid, the ear is unripe. If it oozes thickly, it's past it. If it's milky and sweet, it's ready.

Remove from the stalk by twisting the ear gently. Don't do this until you're ready to race home and cook ASAP. Once picked, the sugars in the kernels convert to starches. If delayed, pop it in the fridge to retard this conversion process. Boil for three minutes only in unsalted water, drain and cool briefly, then tuck in with a dab of butter and black pepper. The cooking water can be

mid-august
harvest versus holidays

It's just not summer without some form of summer holiday. Slavish though I am to my veggies, for my sanity, I still require a break from the city for a while during the warm months. So we pack up our campervan (with a bag full of harvest, naturally) for our annual trip to North Wales, a favourite destination for hiking, chilling and refueling. On our way back, as we bomb down the M1 motorway with a full moon rising towards home, memories of Welsh mountain scenery and relaxing on sprawling sandy beaches shift to make way for eager anticipation about the state of things down at the allotment. Just over a week of neglect at peak cropping season – would it be rack and ruin, or just a bit of a mess of weeds and overgrown vegetables?

Once home, before checking phone messages or emails or opening any post, we head straight to the plot. Pessimism is usually good preparation; one year we returned to a tomato crop completely destroyed by blight, but now we're a bit more savvy and take preventative measures as best we can. There is an embarrassing surfeit of runner beans as expected, a few comically monstrous courgettes and a forest of weeds, but otherwise disaster has been averted and I needn't have worried. You can take the girl out of the allotment, but you can't take the allotment out of the girl.

It's plain that the apogee of high summer has been and gone. Days are noticeably shorter, verdant hues on the plot are making way for more yellows, and some plants look positively scraggly. However, the best is yet to come in the eating department, as those sun-loving plants I started off in the dark cold days of early March finally deliver the goods. It's tomato time!

✳ tomatoes

It's easy to grow what seems like too many tomatoes. The plants can be prolific and reach huge proportions. However, with countless ways of processing toms besides eating raw and making sauce, they're one of your best friends in the kitchen.

They also can last indoors for some time, if necessary. Nothing is lost if tomatoes are stored properly – in fact their flavour might well improve if they are still ripening.

The first sun-warmed, ripe fruits are best enjoyed sliced on a plate, sprinkled with a little salt, torn shreds of basil, mint or oregano scattered over, and a drizzle of olive oil plus a few drops of vinegar.

Tomatoes have an affinity with pasta, but also bread and olive oil. Mediterranean variations on this theme include peasant-style Spanish gazpacho, a chilled puree of tomatoes, bread, olive oil, garlic and vinegar; Catalunyan 'pa amb tomáquet', crusty bread rubbed with garlic and crushed tomato followed by salt and olive oil; and Italian Panzanella, a bread salad.

Opposite Keep picking the tomatoes as they ripen.

pull up onions
Onions and shallots can be pulled and used whenever you need them throughout the growing season, but by this stage they will have mostly flopped over and retired their brown foliage to ground level. Although there is no great urgency, it's time to dry them out for storage for a constant supply over the next few months until they run out. Choose a fine day and ideally a period with a dry forecast. Using a fork, gently lever them from below the surface so they are sitting on top of the soil. Leave them until they have dried out – two days or more, depending on the weather.

Dry them out further by storing them on airy racks, such as greenhouse staging, which may well be available now – but keep the greenhouse well ventilated if you do so. Another good drying method is to get stackable plastic crates from greengrocers, which may have contained mushrooms, fill with your onions and stack them up in a cool dry place. You can plait them into bunches before they dry out completely and hang up, again somewhere cool and dry.

go on holiday!
After all the investment that has gone into cornucopial harvest, it's a great shame to let it all go now, but let's face it, everybody needs to get away and typically summertime is the time to do it. The workload definitely lightens up in August, except on the harvesting and watering front.

If you plan to go away, ask a neighbour or friend to water for you in exchange for whatever produce they care to harvest (and surprise them with a stupendous gift when you return). We leave a rotating sprinkler in the middle of the allotment when we have to go away and ask Ulrika to switch it on if it needs it, while she works at her plot. It's not ideal, as at this time certain plants like tomatoes prefer watering directly on the roots to avoid disease, but it's doing the same job a rain shower would be doing, which is better than nothing. Or, you might consider installing a timer switch to set off the sprinkler automatically, or investing in a soaker hose.

Containers dry out the quickest. It pays to stand them in trays that will retain water. Fill the trays before you leave. Or, reuse empty 2-litre plastic bottles as watering devices. Cut off the bottom, poke holes in the screwcap and reattach, then stick the pouring end in the soil, then fill with water, which will be absorbed relatively slowly. (For more information on watering, see page 16.)

Harvest as much as you possibly can before you go away, and process it, especially for the freezer. The prospect of a holiday is a great motivator to get a lot of processing done. Also you can pick unripe tomatoes and put them on a windowsill, where they will continue to ripen, while the growing plants keep producing more fruits for your return.

also Sow salad onions for fresh growth over winter, directly in the ground or in containers.

Create a strawberry bed now for a harvest next June. Or, if growing in containers, wait to buy the plants until spring.

Keep sowing chard and rocket directly in the ground or containers for autumn and winter harvesting.

Stop harvesting rhubarb so that it can regain its strength for next year.

 summer cabbage

Cabbage is generally regarded as a winter vegetable, but there is a variety for every season. Summer cabbages are usually sown at the same time as winter ones but are ready much earlier. As a result they have less time to develop pest damage and have a more delicate texture and a light fresh flavour, as they haven't had to tough it out through the cold months.

Summer cabbage can be steamed or stir-fried, but usually demands salad. Shred or grate very finely and use it as is, or sprinkle with salt, leave in a colander in the sink to drain for a while, then mix with a little top-quality vinegar, a touch of sugar, and thinly sliced onions. Build on this base, adding tomatoes, olives, peppers, toasted spices such as cumin, or toasted sesame seeds. Finish with a drizzle of olive oil.

Opposite Some onions can be pulled now for immediate use or left to dry off on the soil surface before storage.

late august
BBQ time

At any opportunity, we transport the barbecue to the plot and cook there. We also bring down a box of condiments and eating implements and use the allotment tap for washing veg. Just about everything growing gets its turn over the hot coals – baby beetroot, whole wet garlic bulbs, fat spring onions, young leeks, green chillies and peppers, fennel, courgettes, sweetcorn, even some slices of Alex's windfall apples are surprisingly good BBQ'd, sprinkled with a little sugar. Hot barbecued lettuce – a hearting variety like Romaine – might sound weird but I'm telling you, it's a treat, drizzled with oil, balsamic vinegar and lashings of grated Parmesan. Sometimes I cook a parcel of potatoes wrapped in foil with herbs, placed directly on the coals. A bit earlier in the summer, broad beans get steamed to perfection inside the pod, just tossed on the grill.

This year I'm looking forward to barbecuing my first successful aubergine – they are a very barbie-friendly vegetable, either smoked directly on the coals or sliced and basted on the grill. Yes, I have finally achieved it; after three consecutive years of failure, a fully fruiting 'graffiti' striped aubergine plant. This is entirely down to our makeshift greenhouse. Previous plants were kept in a sheltered, sunny spot, but never produced anything beyond the flowering stage. This is an exciting milestone for me, because I am unnaturally passionate about aubergines. Over the years I have been an aubergine ambassador, extolling the virtues of this misunderstood vegetable and praising its versatility and unique characteristics in cookery demos and on TV shows. To have now created my very own aubergine crop from a tiny seed is cause for celebration.

✳ squash leaves and blossoms

Squash leaves will be dark and leathery by now, but the plants should still be throwing out new shoots. Pick from July onwards to control these domineering plants. Earlier in the season, even larger leaves are tasty, but by late August stick to the small, bright green young ones (see page 98).

Wash all leaves and shred. Fry a generous amount of garlic in oil for 1–2 minutes, add the leaves and a pinch of salt (they shrink considerably so don't overdo the salt). Stir for a couple of minutes, cover and allow to steam in their own juice, stirring occasionally. Depending on size, they may take up to 15 minutes before suitably tender and reduced. Serve hot, with anything, or in solitary splendour. I love this as an appetiser, on its own.

Squash blossoms have had their hey-day by now, but a few will still appear. To prepare, remove the stem and furry stamen. Rinse off any insects. Stuff with mozzarella or ricotta mixed with crushed garlic, roll in seasoned flour and fry in butter, with torn sage leaves.

Opposite A globe artichoke in bloom, passed the edible stage. It's worth leaving some to bloom for their striking display.

Left Sunflowers are gorgeous and attract bees and other friendly pollinators. **Above** A pumpkin ripening happily in situ.

I have yet to try an artichoke on the barbecue, but it's too late now – they've all bloomed into gorgeous giant purple thistles standing seven feet tall. The bees go crazy for them: when they land on the saucer-size shag carpet of purple stamen, they just can't believe their luck and writhe about ecstatically for ages. A couple of inquisitive Turkish ladies passed by the other day and asked me why I had let the artichokes go into flower instead of eating them. I explained that I had feasted on at least one artichoke a day in early summer, but that I'd deliberately left some to bloom into what has to be the most dazzling ornamental plant ever. They recommended I try frying artichoke bottoms in olive oil and adding to an omelette. Note taken.

key jobs right now

final late sowings
Time is just about up for sowing. Not bad as it's been non-stop since early March! Your root veg, brassicas and leeks should keep you supplied over the winter but, if you'd like to try a few things you've not yet grown, this is the last chance. Various exotic greens can be sown now, like pak choi, cima di rapa, mustard leaf, tatsoi and Chinese leaf cabbage, as well as spring cabbages and special types of winter-hardy salad onions and lettuces. See what you can find online, in seed catalogues or in the garden centre. Sow more chard now to be sure you have a plentiful supply over winter. Continue sowing lettuce indoors in trays.

place straw under pumpkins
Pumpkins have swelled quite a bit by now, but still have a way to go, ripening and hardening in situ until October. A bed of straw placed underneath provides ventilation, discouraging deterioration. Straw can be made by drying out grass clippings in the sun, though I buy mine cheap from the pet supplies aisle of a supermarket – ideal for rabbits' hutches and, as it turns out, pumpkins plants too!

podded runner beans

By now, some of your runners may have gone way past the stage where you can eat them green. If they're dangling from the vines bulging with fully formed beans, leave on the vine to dry for a few more weeks until you dismantle the frame, then remove from the brittle pods and store in a jar. Be warned, however, that one year I had a violent allergic reaction to some kind of spore that had formed on the dead plants while doing this.

Once the beans are formed in the pod, they can be extracted and cooked fresh, frozen or dried (soak overnight before cooking from dry). Shuck them by snapping the pod where each bean is. They have a lovely flavour when boiled in salted water until completely soft (5–15 minutes depending on the size) and served with a drizzle of olive oil or melted butter and a few chopped summer herbs. The most remarkable thing about them is their startling hot pink colour which, sadly, goes a rather unappetising shade of grey when cooked.

smoky gazpacho

Gazpacho comes in many guises – this most closely resembles Salmorejo, a cold, thick, rich, salmon-pink gazpacho from the hills of Cordoba, Spain. Traditionally its garnishes include Ibérico ham, but instead I've used fried courgette strips spiked with pimentón. The garnishes are optional, but they do make a meal of the soup. If serving plain, just sprinkle pimentón on top.

1 small or ½ large stale crusty baguette (dry but not mouldy), about 150g

2 tbsp good red wine vinegar or sherry vinegar

100ml water

4 tbsp extra virgin olive oil + 4 more + 2 more

600g ripe tomatoes (about 4 large), roughly chopped

1 small cucumber or ½ large one, peeled and roughly chopped, saving a small 2cm piece for garnish

2 cloves garlic, bitter sprout removed if old, roughly chopped

Large pinch of sea salt and freshly ground black pepper

Optional garnishes

2 hard-boiled organic eggs, finely chopped

2cm piece cucumber, peeled and finely chopped

1 medium courgette

2 tsp pimentón (smoked paprika – sweet or hot, to your taste) + a little extra

Cut or tear the bread into small pieces and place in a bowl. Sprinkle with the vinegar, pour over the water and drizzle over 4 tbsp olive oil. Leave to soften while you prepare the rest of the soup.

In a food processor, combine the tomatoes, cucumber and garlic with a large pinch of salt. Whiz on high power for a couple of minutes, until you have a smooth puree. Add the soaked bread and plenty of pepper and blitz until as smooth as possible, adding the 4 more tbsp olive oil gradually through the feed tube. Taste for seasoning.

Pour the soup into a bowl or large jug, cover and refrigerate for at least two hours to chill and develop flavour. Meanwhile, prepare the garnishes, if using.

To prepare the courgette, trim, cut in half across the middle and then cut again along the seeds into four long pieces. Slice into thin strips. Heat a large frying pan over a medium heat and add 2 tbsp olive oil. Fry the courgette strips until golden and crisp. Remove from the heat, sprinkle in the pimentón and stir to coat. Drain the strips on kitchen paper.

When ready to serve, taste the chilled soup once more for seasoning and stir. Ladle the soup into bowls and sprinkle the garnishes (if using) on top of each: chopped egg in one section, cucumber in another, and fried courgette strips in another. Finish with a final light sprinkle of pimentón. **Serves 4**

Prep tip Cut the tomatoes in half through the stem and cut out the hard flesh around the stem before chopping.

allotment bbq platter with two sauces

Home-grown edibles cooked on the barbecue have endless possibilities. Here are two delicious condiments to go with your garden grills. The Spicy BBQ Sauce can also be used as a marinade or for basting while cooking.

Spicy BBQ Sauce
4 tbsp tomato puree
1 tbsp honey
2 tbsp shoyu or soy sauce
    (light or dark)
2 tbsp cider vinegar
1 tsp pimentón (smoked
    paprika) or regular paprika
1 tsp cumin seed
Large pinch of cayenne
    pepper or to taste
Large handful of fresh
    coriander, stems and
    leaves, roughly chopped
Large handful of parsley
    leaves
1–2 cloves garlic, crushed
    to a paste with a pinch of
    coarse salt in a mortar
2 tbsp olive oil
2 tbsp water

Tahini Sauce
2 heaped tbsp tahini (sesame
    paste)
4 tbsp boiling water
1 clove garlic, crushed to a
    paste with a pinch of coarse
    salt in a mortar
Juice of 1 lemon
2 heaped tbsp natural plain
    yoghurt
Sea salt and freshly ground
    black pepper

For the Spicy BBQ Sauce, simply combine everything in a liquidiser and whiz until smooth. Add a little more water if needed to get the blades moving. **Serves 4**

For the Tahini Sauce, in a small bowl, stir together the tahini and boiling water until smooth. Add the garlic and lemon juice and stir – it may curdle, but just keep stirring and it will smooth out. Stir in the yoghurt and seasoning. (Thin with water if a more dressing-like consistency is preferred.) **Serves 4**

sweetcorn + spiced avocado soup

I wish I could grow my own avocados, but alas, I live in the UK. I will happily buy them in anytime though, especially to create this marriage made in heaven with sweetcorn.

1 tsp whole cumin seed
1 litre water
500ml sweetcorn kernels, stripped from cob (measured by volume; 4 cobs approx – reserve the stripped cobs)
Sea salt and freshly ground black pepper
3 large or 4 medium ripe avocados

Juice of 1 lime
2 spring onions, white and green parts, sliced
2 small red chillies, finely chopped (1 tsp approx – or to taste)
Chopped coriander and yoghurt or crème fraîche, to finish

In a small dry frying pan over a moderate heat, toast the cumin seeds for about 1 minute, until they turn a shade darker. Transfer to a plate or bowl.

Bring the water to a boil in a saucepan. Add the stripped sweetcorn cobs (not the kernels) and simmer for 10 minutes or more to make a stock.

Meanwhile, scrape the avocado flesh into a mixing bowl. Add lime juice and mash to a puree. Add spring onions, chopped chilli and cumin seeds and mash again. Season with salt and black pepper.

Remove the cobs from the stock and add the sweetcorn kernels and salt to taste. Return to a simmer and cook for 2 minutes, until the sweetcorn is just tender. Remove from the heat.

Stir in the avocado mixture and combine well. Taste for seasoning. Serve immediately in warm bowls and top each with chopped coriander and a dollop of yoghurt or crème fraîche. **Serves 4**

Prep tip To strip the sweetcorn kernels, stand a cob on one end in a large bowl. Use a sharp knife to slice the kernels off using a downward motion.

past-it runner beans soup

Once beans can be seen through the pods, they're too stringy to eat. This soup uses them up.

Fry a couple of chopped onions and garlic, then add 1 litre stock or water and bring to the boil. Add 1kg roughly chopped runner beans with salt and pepper, and bring to the boil. Add a bouquet garni of rosemary, thyme and bay leaf tied up with string. Simmer for 20–30 minutes, until the beans are totally soft. Remove the herbs, puree the soup, then push through a sieve. Reheat and serve with a dollop of yoghurt or grated cheese.

slow-roasted tomatoes

One of the easiest ways to process tomatoes is to oven-dry them, concentrating the flavour.

Halve the tomatoes and place cut side up on a baking tray. Sprinkle with chopped garlic, add salt and pepper and drizzle with olive oil and a few drops of balsamic vinegar. Cook at 150°C (300°F) for 1½–2 hours or until done to your liking, cool and eat.

autumn

SEPTEMBER	INDOORS OR UNDER GLASS	OUTDOORS DIRECT IN SOI
Apples		
Aubergines		
Beetroot		
Broccoli (sprouting)		
Brussel sprouts		
Cabbage (summer)		
Carrots		
Cauliflower		
Chard	★	★
Courgettes/summer squashes		
Cucumbers		
Fennel		
Flowers (edible/companion)		
Grapes		
Kale		
Leeks		
Lettuce/salad leaves	★	★
Onions/shallots		
Oriental greens	★	★
Pears		
Peppers and chillies		
Perpetual spinach	★	★
Plums		
Potatoes		
Radishes	★	★
Raspberries		
Rocket	★	★
Runner beans/other beans		
Spinach	★	★
Spring onions	★	★
Strawberries		
Sweetcorn		
Tomatoes		
Turnips		★
Winter herbs		
Winter squashes/pumpkins		

UITABLE FOR CONTAINERS	HARVESTING NOW	RECIPES AND OTHER INFORMATION
★	★	apple + thyme tart + boozy toffee, 150; *see also 147*
★	★	thai smoked aubergine salad, 167; *see also 124, 155*
★	★	*see 138*
★	★	psb + barley risotto, 39; *see also 35*
★	★	zesty brussels sprouts, p203; *see also 27, 42, 195*
★	★	lemony lentil cabbage parcels, 203; *see also 123*
★	★	*see 167, 179*
★	★	cauliflower + coconut soup, 182; *see 172, 183*
★	★	sorrel + chard kuku, 36; *see also 32, 39, 57*
★	★	warm courgette salad, 113; *see also 102, 128, 148*
★	★	smoky gazpacho, 128; *see also 105, 167*
★	★	*see 140*
★	★	*see 116*
★	★	*see 87*
★	★	saffron rice broth + winter greens, 38; *see also 42*
★	★	see 24, 45
★	★	broad beans with lettuce, 75; *see also 57, 63*
★	★	*see 36, 39, 75, 161*
★		*see 181*
★	★	chocolate upright pear cake, 184; *see also 176, 202*
★	★	*see 112, 131, 143, 144*
★	★	*see 32*
★	★	*see 137*
★	★	parmesan potato cakes, 93; *see also 57, 91*
★	★	*see 64*
★	★	*see 108*
★	★	green soup, 57; *see 46*
★	★	soy glazed runner beans, 112; *see also 106, 127, 131*
★	★	*see 32*
★	★	green soup, 57; *see also 61, 72, 92, 112, 131*
★	★	*see 83*
★	★	sweetcorn + spiced avocado soup, 131; *see also 119*
★	★	slow-roasted tomatoes, 131; *see also 120, 158, 166*
★	★	*see 180*
★	★	*see 150, 169, 198*
★	★	pumpkin pasty, 169; *see also 124, 149, 162, 165, 167*

early september
little r.

The harvest is still rolling in, but there's a sense of waning, already. The days are noticeably shorter, the greens are shifting to gold and there's a whispering leaf rustle rolling over the plot. September afternoons can be some of the loveliest of the year, with the sun hanging at a slightly different angle. The resident allotment cats sunbathe languidly, ignoring each other, too lazy to flinch at the unchallenging pigeons or unattainable squirrels. Even slugs and bugs don't seem that bothered. Everything has shifted down a gear. This is the denouement, as chilly nights start drawing in.

However, one particular type of pest persists: the teenage kids who play football in the street just outside the lottie after school. The ball gets kicked over the fence onto our plot regularly, sometimes knocking over a corn stalk or mashing up a lettuce. When we aren't there, the youngest of the gang, who is still just little enough to slip through the bars of our fence, is in charge of fetching it. I've had to train him to respect our space over the last two seasons. A few times I ended up fuming when I found trainer prints on my onions, but I suppressed my annoyance and bribed little R., offering him bags of veg to take to his mum if he's careful not to trample my plants. I've even given him money to buy ice cream from the 'predatory' ice-cream van that pulls up at 4:30 sharp every single afternoon with its deafening 'Yankee Doodle Dandy' jingle.

These days he'll sometimes opt to come and hang out on the plot instead of join the football game. He's always willing to help, but there's not much I can delegate – sweet as he is, he's likely to do more damage than good, and he's got the attention span of a robin. I'll let him choose what he wants to take

Opposite Late summer on plot no. 5.

 plums

I've only ever enjoyed plums vicariously. Alex in Plot No 6 used to have a towering greengage tree, which he felled to get more light on his patch. I miss the windfalls it gushed all over my plot. Although the fallen fruits' nectar attracted wasps, if caught in time, I'd scoop them up and suck the sweet flesh off the stone there and then. There are wild plums to be found in various parks nearby – I've located Mirabelle, Bullace and Damson trees, so I try not to forget my foraging bag when I go for walks from late July to October.

This member of the rose family offers a staggering array of varieties. Small, tart ones with good pectin levels for jam and chutney; sweeter ones better for baking in crumbles, stewing in wine, or best of all, eating raw. Plums love the company of pastry – replace the stone with a sugar lump and chopped almonds, wrap in puff pastry and bake, or for a savoury starter, wrap half a plum in buttered filo layers with goat's cheese, fennel seeds and fronds before baking.

beetroot

This veg has everything going for it. In the garden, it's reliable, relatively pest-free and grows anywhere as it doesn't fall under crop rotation requirements, plus it doesn't mind containers. It keeps in the ground, so has year-round potential. It's two vegetables in one, with flavour-packed leaves and stalks as well as the root. It can be eaten at all stages, from thinning to baby to beast. Raw or cooked, savoury or sweet, it's been elevated to 'superfood' status for its antioxidant and anticarcinogen properties.

If the greens are fresh and lively, cook them as chard or spinach. As for the root, whatever size, leave the spindly part of the root on and cut the leaves at the bottom of the stalks rather than piercing the skin of the root. Scrub well and boil or steam until tender, cool until you can handle it, then rub off the skin. Or roast with a slick of oil and eat skin and all.

Beetroot is a good partner to many things including sharp fruits, blue cheese, walnuts and hazelnuts, coconut, and peppery leaves, such as rocket.

to his mum from a day's harvest, knowing full well that he'll opt for the overgrown courgettes, so that gets those off my hands. He's told me his dad loves the courgettes because they remind him of his childhood in India. His mum is from Bangladesh, and she gives me a nod and a smile through teeth stained by the pan she constantly chews.

On hot summer days, a war of water balloons is likely to be in full swing. Since little R. and a couple of his littler mates are the only ones who can fit through the fence, they've got the upper hand over the teenagers, as I'll let them fill up their balloons from our tap. (I hide the special key that operates the tap when we're not there so I can supervise the artillery when the game is on.) It's a funny way to have earned some street cred, but I think I've got it.

key jobs right now

dig up potatoes
I have usually munched my way through the majority of my potato crop by now, but there are always more to be dug up and stored, at least for the short term. As I've said before, I prefer the flavour of freshly dug potatoes, plus I'm not aiming for complete self-sufficiency, and spuds are cheap enough to buy over the winter, so I don't plant acres of them in the first place. But if there are some remaining, it's time for them to come up this month.

Pull up all the foliage (or haulms) and throw them away, rather than compost, just in case there's any disease lurking. Dig the whole patch, because there are always some that eluded the fork the first time. Bring the spuds to the surface, then let them dry for a couple of days. Finally, store the dry potatoes in a hessian, thick paper or woven plastic bag, allowing for some ventilation. Placing an apple or orange in the bag releases a gas which will help preserve them. Strange but true!

sow green manure These are crops that can be sowed in now vacant patches, like the cleared potato patch, that will give goodness back to the soil, either over a short period or over the winter or longer. These crops are eventually dug into the soil, to further increase fertility once they've completed their nourishing lifespan. They have the added advantage of dominating weeds, which might otherwise take over a vacant patch. It's important to choose the right type of green manure for both the season and length of the growing period, and also the right type for crop rotation. For example, the traditional crop to follow potatoes is mustard, but since mustard is a brassica, you shouldn't follow it with another brassica crop. This information can easily be found online, in detailed gardening manuals or on the seed packets of green manures, which are available from garden centres and seed catalogues.

'Dig the whole patch, because there are always some that eluded the fork the first time.'

Above left Freshly dug 'Desirée' potatoes. **Above right** When digging potatoes it's best not to thrust the fork in too vigorously to avoid impaling the tubers.

mid-september
holding on to summer

As a petulant wind jostles crisp leaves and a spitting rain persists, the smell of a garlic-laden tomato soup bubbling away on the stove is a great comfort. I seem to have a lot more time in the kitchen now as the days are shorter, and I need it! This is prime chutney-making season, and there are a lot of tomatoes to get through. And fennel, and apples, and squashes, and peppers, and… the bounty seems endless, but alas, autumn is undeniably upon us.

So I'm bottling up summer as best I can. Or, to be more precise, freezing it. I'll try and roll out as many soups, pasta sauces, curries, tagines and cheese-laden veggie casseroles as I can muster, to freeze in portions for quick hot lunches and dinners over the coming months. The instant gratification of a ready-to-heat home-grown dish is a godsend in winter. These get used up faster than individually frozen vegetables, some of which don't quite match their just-picked flavour once frozen. However, broad beans, peas, runner beans, chard and broccoli freeze particularly well and are always a welcome addition to a quick hot udon noodle broth. Potatoes which have been boiled, crushed and frozen in portions are also very handy for a fry-up.

Two or three batches of contrasting allotment chutneys a year are a must, primarily to give away as Christmas presents, secondarily for our own enjoyment – in winter our cheese and biscuit consumption accelerates, especially if there's an open jar of chutney on the go. As for other bottling, perhaps I'll make the odd pickled something or other and a bit of jam, but I'm more of a freezer queen myself. In fact I might be considered rather cavalier in the preserving department, as I've given up spending money on fancy rubber-ringed preserving jars. I just save all sorts of ordinary food jars with metal lids through the year, soak the

✳ fennel

Bulb or Florence fennel is a real treat. It's fairly easy to grow. Start off from seed from late March to June in small pots indoors or in the greenhouse, then transplant outside or into large containers when about 7–10cm tall. It can also be sown directly in the soil. Snails and slugs are lured to the strong aniseed fragrance of baby fennel, so protect young seedlings.

Fennel may bolt if there's a fluctuation in temperature – if this happens, harvest right away. Or let it go and enjoy it for the chartreuse flowers. The blooms are a visual feast, and on the plate, they are delicious sautéed or fried in batter. If left to form seeds, these are a flavour sensation, fresh or dried (see page 156).

Fennel roots are worth scrubbing and cooking, tasting like their sister the parsnip. The outer bulb layers are coarse and gritty, but don't discard – they add a delicate flavour to soup stock, as do the feathery fronds. Boil in salted water with an onion or two, then strain.

Above Chillies strung up by their stems using a needle and thread, drying in the window at home. **Right** The annual chutney in recycled screwtop jars.

labels off, wash them and run them through the dishwasher. I then sterilise and seal them in the usual way: arrange them in a baking tray on a few sheets of kitchen paper, heat the oven to 180°C and pop the jars into the oven for at least 10 minutes. To sterilise the lids, I place them in a saucepan, cover with water and bring to the boil – they ought to be boiled for 10 minutes or so. I then drain and dry them thoroughly. It's free, it's recycling, and it works for my chutneys.

key jobs right now

ventilate the greenhouse Peppers,
chillies and aubergines will still be appreciating the magnified heat of the greenhouse when the sun comes out, but so will pests that are sensing the imminent change of season. Keeping the greenhouse and coldframe open for a while during the daytime should help stop fungal diseases and pests getting established there.

winter plans There are a few more planting
opportunities coming up before winter sets in, so now is a good time to do any catalogue or online ordering. Fruit bushes and trees can go in the ground next month, as can over-wintering broad beans, garlic and onions. Early winter will be the time for manuring if you are going down that road, so find a source now, or any other well-rotted compost you can get your hands on.

Opposite Our homemade greenhouse constructed from discarded plastic sheeting gets extra ventilation during September.

 chillies

By now chilli plants should be sporting their racing stripes when ripe; some are orange, purple, yellow or even white, not just red and green. They come in a bewildering array of shapes, sizes and heat levels. Some plants are ornamental – one year I grew a Korean variety that was still lush with dangling red fruits at Christmas time – so that became our Christmas tree that year.

Chillies are indispensable in my kitchen. My catering-size box of latex gloves gets used for veg prep of all types but is essential for handling chillies.

Even the staunchest chilli-lover is likely to overuse it in cooking at some point. Water won't quell the burn. It is, however, inhibited by sugar, alcohol, some fats, and casein (a protein in milk). Drinking beer might help a little, but tequila is a better bet; otherwise juice, a spoonful of sugar or yoghurt or a glass of milk should speed recovery. It is no coincidence that sour cream accompanies Mexican food, yoghurt accompanies Indian food, and Thai food is full of sugar.

late september
autumn undeniable

It's now official – summer is over. But the trug continues to fill daily. Actually I don't use a trug – it's far too impractical, pretentious and small. Plastic carrier bags do the job perfectly, then get reused for lining the kitchen compost container. For a while I was using biodegradable container liners, but found them too leaky. I also made an effort to avoid acquiring any plastic bags from the local shops or supermarket (a place I almost never go) by bringing my own cloth ones, until I realised that I actually need a few plastic carrier bags in my life. Not millions, but a few. OK, they're generally not biodegradable, but they do several jobs. At least I have my plastic bag consumption under control.

The new kid on the block crop-wise right now is a swathe of juicy purple Cypriot grapes, from a vine we inherited from a plot-holder of years gone by. I call it Cypriot because we have one at home too, which extends from our next door neighbour's garden – he brought it over from his native Cyprus – and the vine on the plot produces identical grapes. We use the tender leaves in late spring and early summer, as did many local passers-by (the vine draped itself over the fence facing the street, see page 87). Now the grapes themselves are ripe, and they are incredible – small and pippy, but intensely sweet and staining. I've tried pressing the juice out of them and freezing it in ice-cube trays, for popping into sauces and so on, but it's so sugary that it refuses to freeze. I guess they are crying out to be made into jelly or wine, but meanwhile we just eat them, pips and all, and laugh at our blue tongues afterwards.

✳ sweet peppers

In a greenhouse, cold frame, or sheltered patio or balcony, you may have had success with a few sweet capsicums which should be ripening now. Like their chilli cousins, they are available in a baffling number of varieties and present themselves as a gorgeous ornamental plant.

Home-grown peppers will always be irregular and possibly rather sparse in quantity unless you have lots of warm space for many plants, but they are so much more delicious than the watery store-bought specimens. It's a thrill to watch them develop and change colour as they sweeten in the sunbeams over several weeks, then to harvest them and enjoy the complex flavour, one or two at a time.

Slice them raw into salads or use in chutney. Roasted peppers are one of the last hurrahs of summer and they taste incredible: slice in half, remove the seeds and roast or grill skin-side to the flame until black and blistered all over, scrape into a plastic bag while hot and leave to cool, then peel. After this treatment they can also be frozen.

Opposite A fraction of the season's tomato harvest.

bid farewell to tomatoes

At the end of September or beginning of October, frost might be around the corner. Even in a concrete jungle, temperatures may become inhospitable for plants, but they've done their duty, so it's time to finish off the tomato crop, now or within a week or so. Fortunately, you can continue to ripen fruits indoors. Snip the green fruit-laden trusses off the plant. Stretch a string somewhere inside – kitchen, bedroom, shed, anywhere you have space – and hang the trusses from it, securing with clothes pegs if necessary. Natural gasses emitted by ripe fruits encourages the green ones to ripen. Any really under-developed ones will never get there, but can still be eaten cooked or used in chutney (see pages 148 and 167). Pull up the remains of the plants and dismantle any frame or supports used. Rather than compost, discard the plants in case there are any traces of blight present.

compost finished crops

Cold nights may have finished off many crops by now, leaving pale remnants of their former selves. If your sweetcorn is finished, pull up the stalks and chop them up into the compost heap – these provide good fibrous matter for the heap. Any peas or beans left on the plot should be hacked down at the base, leaving the roots to nourish the soil, and the rest composted. Pumpkin and squash plants, with their abundance of leaves and tendrils, will be ready for the heap as well. If there are any new green leaves still coming, by all means harvest them for cooking (see page 124). Cut the maturing pumpkins from the plants, leaving a thumb-length of stem attached. Pumpkins can be moved to a sunny spot to continue ripening, or brought inside.

also

Order some garlic seed stock for planting out in late October or early November (see page 175).

Opposite top My plot neighbour Alex's tasty apples. **Opposite bottom** Green 'Rainbow Beefsteak' cordon tomatoes, ready to cook or ripen indoors.

apples

With modern dwarf rootstocks, you can have an apple tree in even the tiniest of gardens. I'm reliant on my plot neighbours, my mother-in-law, and wild trees in the nature reserves of London for my apple supply. You won't catch me with an apple flown over from New Zealand, though I'll happily pay for British varieties in season. This is one of the crops that instils great British pride. All types of Pippins and Russets are my favourites – crisp, juicy and explosively sweet-sour.

The wind provides a generous supply of apples, dropping onto my plot from my neighbour Alex's tree, which I claim before some other critter does. Apples don't store well if they've been bruised falling from the tree. Mostly I eat them, but a few go into my Harvest Chutney (see page 148), as well as finding their way into soup with fennel or carrots, and even the occasional potato gratin. Good strong Cheddar cheese and apples is a match made in heaven. Or they'll go into one of my favourite autumn desserts (see page 150).

harvest chutney

Preserve your hard-earned produce in jars. Use whatever is to hand to make up the 3kg weight; just make sure there's some fruit and a representative of the onion family in the mix. Multiple the recipe as necessary.

3kg allotment produce, hand-chopped into medium chunks (whole shelled hazelnut size) – for example, roughly equal quantities of green tomatoes, peeled apples, and courgettes, plus about 5–10 onions, 12 cloves of garlic, and 8 medium-hot green chillies, to make up the pre-chopped 3kg weight

2 tbsp sea salt

2 tbsp mixed whole spices (such as coriander seeds, dill seeds, fennel seeds, mustard seeds, cumin seeds, nigella seeds, cloves)

8 bay leaves

750g golden granulated sugar or soft brown sugar

500ml cider vinegar, wine vinegar or white distilled malt vinegar (5% acidity minimum – check the label)

Preserving jars with rubber rings, or saved and prepared screwtop jars (see page 141)

Place the chopped produce in your widest, heavy-bottomed stainless steel preserving pan with the salt, spices and bay leaves and bring to the boil. Simmer for 20 minutes to release the juices, then add the sugar and vinegar. Return to the boil, reduce the heat to a low simmer and cook until very thick, stirring frequently as the sugar can easily burn on the bottom. This will take somewhere between an hour and 4 hours, depending on the water content of the produce – it needs to reduce until the mixture is thick and jammy – ideally a spoon scraped across the bottom of the pan will leave a clear canal (unless you are making a huge quantity). It is paramount that excess liquid is evaporated for the chutney to be properly preserved.

Shortly before the chutney is done, sterilise the jars (see page 141). Cool the chutney briefly (5–10 minutes), then spoon into the hot jars to fill nearly to the top. Using a towel to hold the hot jars, screw on the dry sterilised lids as tightly as possible.

Leave in a cool, dry place until Christmas or for about 2 months minimum. **Makes about 8 x 200ml jars**

spiced cornmeal-crusted squash blossoms

Male blossoms are the ones with stems, rather than attached to the fruit. They are larger, tastier and easier to stuff. This recipe is inspired by the cuisine of Native Americans in southwest USA, for whom squash blossoms have special ritual signficance.

12 squash, pumpkin or courgette blossoms, prepared as below (see prep tip)
100g soft cream cheese

2 organic eggs
4 tbsp milk

½ tsp cayenne pepper or other chilli powder
½ tsp ground cumin
½ tsp salt

About 100g cornmeal (coarse polenta)
Sunflower oil for frying

Open each blossom carefully and use a teaspoon to fill each one with a little cream cheese, enclosing the cheese completely with the petals.

In a shallow bowl, beat the eggs with the milk, spices and salt until evenly combined. Place the cornmeal in another shallow bowl next to it.

Dip each stuffed blossom in the egg mixture, coating well, then coat each one in cornmeal, gently dredging them until completely covered, carefully pressing them slightly flat without releasing the cheese stuffing. Set aside to a plate. Chill the blossoms for 15–20 minutes. Preheat the oven to warm.

Prepare a large plate with crumpled kitchen paper for draining the blossoms. Heat a large frying pan over a medium heat and pour in a shallow pool of oil. When the oil is hot, fry the blossoms in batches until golden brown on each side, using tongs to turn them. Drain on the kitchen paper, then keep them warm in the oven until all are cooked. Serve as soon as possible. **Serves 4**

Prep tip Rinse the blossoms inside and out under a gentle stream of cold water, then pat dry with kitchen paper. Use scissors to snip out the yellow stamen attached to the base inside the petals – it can taste bitter. Leave a short length of the stem on.

fresh + simple tomato sauce

An easy way to process a bunch of ripe tomatoes.

Fill a saucepan with whole tomatoes of all sizes and shapes. Add salt, a spoonful or two of brown sugar, a splash of wine vinegar, a few whole cloves of garlic and a dash of water. Cover and bring to the boil. Simmer for about 30 minutes, crushing the burst tomatoes half way through cooking. Cool briefly, then puree and push through a sieve. Adjust the seasoning. Reheat and serve, or cool completely, then freeze in portion-sized sealed bags.

apple and thyme tart with boozy toffee

Apple and thyme are extremely happy bedfellows, mingling in a buttery brandy sauce in this classic dessert, a simplified version of the classic Tarte Tatin.

30g slightly salted butter
50g dark brown sugar
40ml whipping cream
2 tbsp brandy or Calvados

1 packet ready-rolled puff
  pastry (about 375g), chilled
Butter for greasing tin
1 tbsp caster sugar
A handful of thyme, leaves
  stripped
6 or 7 small tart apples,
  peeled, halved and cored

A 20cm cake tin with a
  removeable base
Baking parchment

Prep tip Use a long peeler, rather than a D-shaped one, to peel the apples, then cut in half top to bottom. Slice off the ends, then use the sharp end of the peeler to carefully gouge out the cores. Alternatively, use an apple coring tool to get the cores out before cutting in half.

First, make the boozy toffee sauce. Place the butter, sugar and cream in a saucepan and heat together over a moderate heat, stirring until bubbling. Reduce the heat and allow to simmer for about 2 minutes, then remove from the heat. Once it stops bubbling, stir in the booze. Pour into a heat-proof bowl and allow to cool completely.

When ready to cook, preheat the oven to 220°C (425°F). Use the cake tin base as a stencil to cut the pastry into a circle. Place on a plate and keep chilled. Line the base of the tin with baking parchment. Grease the paper and the tin well and sprinkle the caster sugar over the base, swirling to coat evenly. Sprinkle thyme leaves over the base, then place the prepared apples on top, round side down, arranging them nestled together with as few gaps as possible, except a bit around the outside edge.

Place the pastry over the apples and tuck in around the edges inside the pan, so that the pastry edge meets the base of the tin. Place on a baking tray, pop in the oven and cook for 20 minutes, until puffed and golden.

Remove from the oven and leave to cool for at least 15 minutes. Remove the outside of the tin, leaving the upside-down tart on the base. Now, be careful, because the hot liquid released from the apples will slosh out and can burn. Standing over a sink, place a large serving plate upside down over the top of the tart and flip over. Remove the paper and slide the tart off the base and onto the plate. Spoon the cooled toffee sauce evenly over the apples. Cut into wedges and serve warm or cold.
Serves 6–8

OCTOBER	INDOORS OR UNDER GLASS	OUTDOORS DIRECT IN SOIL
Apples		
Aubergines		
Beetroot		
Broad beans		★
Broccoli (sprouting)		
Brussel sprouts		
Cabbage (winter)		
Carrots		
Cauliflower		
Celeriac		
Chard	★	
Cucumbers		
Fennel		
Fruit trees		★
Garlic		★
Grapes		
Kale		
Leeks		
Lettuce/salad leaves	★	
Oriental greens	★	★
Pears		
Peppers and chillies		
Perpetual spinach	★	
Potatoes		
Radishes		
Raspberries		
Rocket	★	
Runner beans/other beans		
Spinach	★	
Spring onions	★	★
Swedes		
Tomatoes		
Turnips		
Winter squashes/pumpkins		
Winter herbs		

UITABLE FOR CONTAINERS	HARVESTING NOW	RECIPES AND OTHER INFORMATION
★	★	apple + thyme tart + boozy toffee, 150; *see also* 147
★	★	thai smoked aubergine salad, 167; *see also* 124, 155
★	★	*see* 138
★		broad bean tabbouleh, 92; *see also* 68, 75, 113
★	★	psb + barley risotto, 39; *see also* 35
★	★	zesty brussels sprouts, p203; *see also* 27, 42, 195
★	★	hot + sour swede + cabbage salad, 200; *see also* 191
★	★	*see* 167, 179
★	★	cauliflower + coconut soup, 182; *see* 172, 183
★	★	celeriac gratin + ceps, 182; *see also* 175
★	★	sorrel + chard kuku, 36; *see also* 32, 39, 57
★	★	smoky gazpacho, 128; *see also* 105, 167
★	★	*see* 140
★		*see* 181
★		broad bean + garlic purée; *see also* 39, 55, 75, 100
★	★	*see* 87
★	★	saffron rice broth + winter greens, 38; *see also* 42
★	★	*see* 24, 45
★	★	broad beans with lettuce, 75; *see also* 57, 63
★	★	*see* 181
★	★	chocolate upright pear cake, 184; *see also* 176, 202
★	★	*see* 112, 131, 143, 144
★	★	*see* 32
★	★	parmesan potato cakes, 93; *see also* 57, 91
★	★	*see* 64
★	★	*see* 108
★	★	green soup, 57; *see* 46
★	★	soy glazed runner beans, 112; *see also* 106, 127, 131
★	★	*see* 32
★	★	green soup, 57; *see also* 61, 72, 92, 112, 131
★	★	hot + sour swede + cabbage salad, 200; *see also* 197
★	★	slow-roasted tomatoes, 131; *see also* 120, 158, 166
★	★	*see* 180
★	★	*see* 150, 169, 198
★	★	pumpkin pasty, 169; *see also* 124, 149, 162, 165, 167

early october
summer's leftovers

In this era of climate change, the weather is increasingly unpredictable, but one thing is certain: October is the month when the Grim Reaper strikes certain specimens on the plot, and the Harvest Reaper must get very busy indeed.

You get hints of it for a couple of weeks before suddenly, whoosh – the temperature slides down a slippery slope. Foliage turns yellow and flattens, but even those plants which are withering are desperately eeking out produce in a last gasp – the final courgettes, a few puny runner beans, some faintly orange tomatoes – even the strawberries are offering up a few pale fruits. The rhubarb has bowed out in listless surrender, but some sallow shoots are still trying to emerge at the core. The root veg don't seem the least bit bothered, and the cabbage patch is revving up for plot domination.

Frost is imminent, so whatever is left that's ripe for eating in the summer veg department needs to be harvested as soon as possible. I grabbed a sunny afternoon to furiously gather green tomatoes, sweetcorn, the final courgettes and leaves from the plants. The last of the maincrop potatoes were brought to the surface and left to dry out a bit. I loaded up the wheelbarrow with pepper, chilli and aubergine plants in pots in a rescue operation, bringing them to their retirement suite in my living room. I was happy to retreat to the warm kitchen for a chutney-making session.

Opposite Last of the summer harvest, including an Oriental radish, garlic chive flowers, cucumbers, courgettes with leaves and blossoms, and sweetcorn.

aubergines

Aubergines are quite happy growing in containers, but in the UK almost certainly need indoor or greenhouse conditions to thrive. For the best crop, one plant should be allowed to produce only 4 or 5 fruits and the rest of the flowers should be removed. Pick the fruits before they over-mature. Ripeness is usually indicated by white (not green) shiny skin underneath the calyx, and like an avocado, the flesh should just give slightly when pressed near the stem. Better to pick them too early than too late; ripening continues off the plant.

Home-grown aubergines have a delicate flavour, but proper cooking is a must – undercooked aubergine is not nice. They are superb roasted: quarter lengthways, score the flesh with diagonal slashes, brush generously with olive oil and roast until golden – wonderful served with crumbled feta, chopped mint and some sweet-sour juice or syrup drizzled over, such as fresh pomegranate juice of molasses.

home-grown spices

Coriander is a favourite herb. I sow it successionally so I have a constant supply of leaf, but it doesn't stop there. The leaf has the weakest flavour of the plant – there's even more in the stems and roots, if used before it bolts and becomes tough. Once bolted, however, after the display of delicate white flowers comes the juicy green globe-shaped seed.

I could grow this herb for the seeds alone, especially when young and green, exploding with an intense, exotic perfume. Once they take on a reddish hue, the seeds get a little bitter, so I leave them to dry off on the plant, then harvest and use as dried coriander spice, ground or crushed.

I throw the green seeds into curries and stir-fries – even just a spoonful adds a wild dimension of flavour. If fennel and dill is left to go to seed, these are also well worth eating fresh or collecting dried. Coriander, fennel and dill seed, as well as the leafy herbs, are all great partners for cooked aubergines.

bring sun-loving plants indoors If they are still productive, plants in pots like peppers, aubergines and tomatoes and also basil should now come in from the cold. Outdoor tomatoes will not be happy about the chilly nights, so it's best to snip off any trusses of fruit and bring them in. Use as necessary. Most of the green ones will slowly ripen in the company of the others, and the presence of an over-ripe banana will speed things up. Hang them from a string suspended in a window, or lined up side-by-side but not touching on a windowsill. Or store them in a drawer or a box in a larder, again not touching, in case one starts to go off and afflicts the others.

tend brassicas As the temperature drops and there is less and less to eat for the pigeons, they will be on the rampage for the brassicas, so keep the plants well protected with fleece or netting even if they are a good size by now. Install a creative scarecrow – make a wooden cross, pound it in near the brassicas and dress it with some disposable garments. Every little helps! Also remove any yellowing leaves from the plants as they appear over the winter.

also Bring your pumpkins and squashes indoors before frost strikes and store somewhere cool and dry. At my house, due to limited space, they often end up in the living room around the fireplace – it's as good a place as any and they are a joy to look at.

Think about buying fruit trees to plant in November if you want a permanent occupant for a certain vacant space.

Collect fallen leaves in black plastic bags for leaf mould compost.

Opposite top Flowering basil plants, varieties including Greek, lemon and cinnamon basil, at home in the kitchen window. **Opposite bottom** Cherry tomato plants on their last legs.

mid-october
harvest festival and the rock 'n' roll vicar

The allotment is situated opposite the vicarage of a rather handsome Victorian gothic church. Opposite the church is a mosque, which occupies a building formerly belonging to the church. Carloads of (mostly) men regularly park outside the plot on their way to the mosque, and they are often very friendly and chatty, enquiring about the plot and my crops as they pass.

A couple of evenings per month, the mosque hosts Sufi meditation circles. Sufi muslims practise chanting and dancing as part of their worship. They arrive wearing elegant emerald green robes with green headscarves and cone-shaped skullcaps. Once I turned on my sprinkler just as a bunch of these finely dressed young gentlemen exited their car – they weren't too badly doused and were very good humoured about it, but I was mortified. We got to chatting, and they warmly invited me join them in a Sufi dancing ritual sometime, an offer which I haven't yet taken up, but really must – it's just the kind of opportunity that might never had arisen were it not for my esoterically positioned allotment, and the way it connects me with my community.

The vicar of the Anglican church, John, lives directly across from the plot with his wife Rena and their two small children. They are the grateful recipients of bags of surplus veg when it comes to pass – Rena is from Uganda and is always keen to whip up a veg curry or some samosas, especially when her mum is visiting and lending a hand with the kids. They keep a close eye on our plot for us, which is dead handy. Rena has been known to tell off the naughty kids who play in the street between our plot and their house, warning them, "Watch out... I know your parents!", when their football

✳ green tomatoes

There are always some green tomatoes left at the end of season. While it is possible to ripen most of them if you have the patience (see page 147), some of them will never get there, as they are immature as opposed to under-ripe. Green tomatoes are a unique fruit in their own right. They are firm and tart and don't collapse as readily as ripe tomatoes in cooking. This makes them perfect for chunky chutney, and also for frying.

Fry slices or wedges in oil, adding salt, pepper and a dash of sugar and vinegar at the end, allowing it to caramelise in the pan, finishing with chopped garlic and herbs if desired – delicious for breakfast with eggs and buttered toast.

There couldn't be an easier or tastier recipe than the classic dish from the southern USA, fried green tomatoes (see page 167).

Opposite End of harvest sweetcorn, runner beans, tomatoes, fennel with its tasty root and a scented rose.

Above and right Asparagus ferns will turn completely yellow by mid Autumn and should be cut down.

'Spent corn stalks and the cut foliage of asparagus, fennel and bright lights chard make regal arrangements.'

antics pose a threat to my crops. John is quite a rock 'n' roll vicar, as vicars go – he wears a leather biker jacket, but he gave up the motorcycle when the little ones came along. His dad was a bishop, and he confesses that he rather languidly followed in the family footsteps, unlike his wild child brother who's a West End stage singer and dancer.

Each year in the middle of October, the church holds a harvest festival. The congregation brings in food to give to charity the week before. For the last three years running, John has asked me if I could make a display for the altar from the allotment, so it's not all baked bean tins and chocolate bars, and I have enthusiastically obliged by loading up the wheelbarrow with some of the faded summer's trophies. Spent corn stalks and the cut foliage of asparagus, fennel, and bright lights chard make regal arrangements along with a pumpkin or two, some root veg and a few roses from the bush. It's a fitting farewell to the growing season.

key jobs right now

cut down asparagus ferns
Once the wall of feathery asparagus ferns turns yellow, it's time to cut them back. Leave stumps about 3–7cm above ground. Give the patch a thorough weeding and apply a layer of compost.

bye-bye beanframe
Your climbing beans can be left happily to dry out on the frame for as long as you like, but by now you may want to disassemble the rather sad-looking mess. Also if you want to reuse the beanpoles, store them in a dry place over winter. The beans' roots will still be doing the soil some good though, so cut them off at the base and compost the spent growth. Any dried-up pods remaining on the plant should contain perfectly good dried beans which you can save to soak and cook, or to replant next year.

also
Prepare a patch for your new allium crop by digging in some compost. It's nearly time to plant garlic and over-wintering onions.

Get a patch ready for a row of over-wintering broad beans (see page 30).

Keep collecting fallen leaves in black plastic bags for leaf mould compost.

onions and shallots

Onions are the flavour foundation of good food, especially vegetable-centric cuisine. Just the smell of an onion frying switches on the appetite and lures people to the kitchen, salivating. As I've said before, you can never have too many onions.

Home-grown onions can be noticeably stronger when pulled fresh from the ground, and thus more tear-inducing when cut. Reputed remedies for this affliction include turning on an electric fan, lighting a candle, and holding a silver spoon in the mouth. Shallots have a slightly milder, sweeter flavour.

Don't add salt to onions when frying as this draws out too much moisture and makes them tough and papery. The slower you fry them, the sweeter they become. Adding a spoonful of sugar and raising the heat towards the end of cooking quickly caramelises them. Try roasting onions and shallots in or out of their skins, with thyme, a little vinegar, seasoning and oil.

✳ pumpkins

Any large, round, hard-skinned squash with fully developed seeds can be classified as a pumpkin. They're not always orange – I've grown a Caribbean variety since my first season, recycling the seeds each time – the flesh is orange but the skin is light green. If a pumpkin feels heavy for its size, it is likely to have dense, velvety flesh, which is the best sort for cooking, giving inimitable texture as well as complex sweet flavour. Pumpkins and most winter squashes store incredibly well – have them as part of your Christmas dinner or beyond.

Tackle pumpkins with a sturdy knife and a strong arm: cut downwards through the stalk first, then in half. Scrape out the seeds and membranes with a spoon and save them, either for eating (see page 167) or re-planting.

Cut the pumpkin into wedges. It's best to remove the skin before cooking. To do this, cut downwards around the edge of each wedge. Coat the wedges in oil and roast for the best flavour.

late october
putting the lottie to bed

I frequently give the plot a glance if I'm passing, just to check up on it. As I'm gazing through the fence poles, an older gentleman passes me and says, "Gosh, some people have really let their plots go here, haven't they?" He had just walked past my neighbour Fred's plots, which are immaculate, manicured, raked to a fine tilth and weed-free, and then he happened on ours. It's true, compared to Fred's, our plot is a disgrace. The days are so short and cold now, and I've been a little lazy in tidying up. Slightly mortified by the stranger's comment, I'm determined to rise early the next day and crack on.

So, as British Summer Time ends, so does a raft of crop remains. It seems an appropriate juncture and I attack it with ceremonious zeal. I pluck off the final clutch of runner beans and dismantle the bean frame, which leaves a gaping hole in the lottie-scape. Crusty sunflowers, diaphanous rhubarb leaves and the skeletal squash plants all make their last journey to the compost bin.

I'm considering building a 'bee hotel' or 'habitat wall' to serve as a winter refuge for friendly insects – I've seen some magnificent examples online. Apparently hollow stalks, twigs, straw, pine cones, stones, and all manner of dried-up garden waste can be put to use welcoming insects that will enrich my urban wilderness. While many bees and insects will have already established their winter abode, some are still looking for shelter. Others will arrive in spring to lay their eggs and I could be ready for them with a harvest hostel, so I'm putting aside some suitable material, before pursuing my internet research on how it's done.

Opposite Some dried up broad bean plants go in the compost bin; others are salvaged for my planned 'bee hotel'.

Above Plait red onions together once dried. **Left** A few twiggy bits are good for the texture of the compost, but don't overdo it.

sow over-wintering broad beans

Although extremely slow in coming, these are a reminder that spring is on its way at a time when winter seems interminable. The claim is that over-wintering broad bean plants have a better chance of being blackfly-free than spring plantings, but so far I have been let down by this theory. Nothing is 100% guaranteed – if the weather is very wet, there is a risk of the seed beans rotting before they germinate, or getting eaten by something or other, but you can sow a few extra indoors in peat pots or toilet rolls just in case (see pages 30–31). Cloches are a good idea once the young plants emerge.

carve a jack-o-lantern

As an American ex-pat, an annual ritual for me is carving a Jack-o-lantern on Hallowe'en night. Depending on how successful the home-grown pumpkin crop is from year to year, Dan pleads with me not to sacrifice one of our own. The best pumpkin for carving is a big round orange one with pale watery flesh and a relatively thin skin, making it easy to carve. This type is scarcely edible anyway compared to its hard-skinned, dense-fleshed relatives, so it's better off serving the purpose of a lantern.

So whether you buy one in for this purpose or use one you grew, it's a fun use for this awesome hollow round vegetable. Wrap foil around the underside of the lid to stop the candle from burning the pumpkin. If it's a good specimen for eating, rinse it and use it in cooking, ideally the day after Hallowe'en. Or there's the rather eccentric pleasure of watching its expression shrivel as it perishes in the garden over the coming weeks, ultimately resulting in fine compost fodder.

also Keep collecting fallen leaves in black plastic bags for leaf mould compost.

Plait dried onions and hang in a cool dark place.

winter squashes

Rather confusingly, these are any other hard-skinned, seed-bearing squashes which may or may not be round, such as butternut, acorn, kaboucha and onion squash. Crown prince is a lovely variety, sometimes called both pumpkin and squash. These should all be treated like pumpkins in preparation and use.

The exception is spaghetti squash, which has delicious stringy flesh that can be forked out like spaghetti once cooked. Pierce the vegetable a few times (don't forget this step or you risk a very messy explosion) and bake whole in a moderate oven until completely tender, or microwave on high for about 5 minutes per 500g, until the skin can be pierced easily and the squash is collapsing. Cool thoroughly, halve lengthways, gently scoop out the seeds with a spoon, then use a fork to pull the strands away from the skin into a bowl. Reheat, then stir in butter and salt, or a rich tomato sauce, or even pesto, and top with cheese.

green tomato curry

A quick, zingy South-Indian-style curry. Adding halved chillies is common in that part of the world – it gives the dish a subtle overall kick, but allows those who love chillies to nibble on the fiery pods.

1 tsp fresh or dried coriander seeds
2 tsp cumin seeds
4 cloves garlic (remove the bitter sprout from the middle, if old)
Pinch of coarse sea salt

4 tbsp virgin rapeseed or sunflower oil
50g raw cashew nuts
1 tsp brown mustard seeds
2 large onions, finely sliced (about 400g)
600g green tomatoes, cut in medium wedges
2cm piece fresh ginger, finely chopped
1 tsp turmeric
3 tbsp unsweetened dessicated coconut
3–4 small fresh red chillies, halved from stem to base
Sea salt and freshly ground black pepper

250ml plain natural yoghurt
Boiled rice and coriander leaves, to serve

Place the coriander seeds, cumin seeds, garlic and salt in a mortar and crush to a paste. Set aside.

Get a small plate ready with crumpled kitchen paper for draining the cashews. Heat a wok or a large wide pan over a medium high heat. Add the oil and then the cashews and stir until golden (this may take only a matter of seconds). Remove from the pan with a slotted spoon and drain on the kitchen paper.

Return the pan to the heat and add the mustard seeds. As soon as they start to pop, add the onions. Fry briskly until the onions are soft, golden and nicely caramelised.

Add the green tomatoes and fry for 3–5 minutes, until lightly coloured. Then add the ginger, turmeric, coconut, chillies, salt and pepper. Stir, then add the garlic mixture. Stir for a couple more minutes until fragrant, then remove the pan from the heat. Quickly stir in the yoghurt until evenly combined, then cover the pan and let it stand for 2 minutes. Taste for seasoning, then serve the curry over rice, topped with the fried cashews and decorated with coriander leaves. **Serves 4–6**

thai smoked aubergine salad

If you like the flavour of authentic baba ganoush, you'll love these smoky aubergines, cooked over a naked gas flame. Alternatively, smoke them on a gas or charcoal bbq.

For the salad
2 medium aubergines

1 small avocado
250g cherry tomatoes, halved
½ red onion, finely sliced
½ cucumber, halved and finely sliced
1 large carrot, peeled and julienned or grated
Large handful of fresh mint, leaves stripped
Handful of coriander, leaves stripped, stems chopped

2 stalks lemon grass, finely sliced (optional)
2 kaffir lime leaves, finely sliced (optional)

2 handfuls toasted cashew nuts, roughly chopped

For the dressing
4 tbsp light soy sauce
4 tbsp fresh lime juice
3 tbsp soft brown sugar
1 clove garlic, crushed
1–2 red or green chillies, finely chopped

First, smoke the aubergines. Push an all-metal fork into the stems and place the body directly onto a high gas flame. Turn occasionally until completely soft and collapsed; the skin should be blackened to the point of ash in places, and steam should be escaping through the fork holes. Remove to a plate and cool. If you find the flavour too assertive or don't cook on gas, simply roast the aubergines in the oven: pierce several times and bake at 220°C (425°F) in a baking dish until soft and collapsed.

When cool enough to handle, chop off the stem of the aubergines and peel off the charred skin. A few remaining blackened bits will add to the flavour. Pull apart into several long strips and set aside.

To make the dressing, mix all ingredients together thoroughly, dissolving the sugar completely.

When ready to serve, cut the avocado in half and remove the stone, then scoop the flesh from the skin with a teaspoon into chunks, or peel and slice. Arrange with the remaining salad ingredients, except cashews, on a platter or individual plates. Pour the dressing over the salad, then top with cashews. **Serves 4**

fried green tomatoes

There couldn't be an easier or tastier recipe for green tomatoes than this classic dish from the southern USA.

Slice larger green tomatoes about 1cm thick. Dredge each slice first in flour, shaking off any excess, then in a bowl of beaten egg, then in seasoned polenta (cornmeal) to coat evenly. Fry in batches, turning over with tongs, until golden and crisp on both sides. Drain on kitchen paper, sprinkle with salt and serve hot.

pumpkin seeds

Munch on these as a snack or sprinkle on salads or on top of pumpkin soup as a crunchy garnish.

Place the seeds with their membranes in a colander and rinse, separating them as well as you can from the fibres using your fingertips. Dry them on kitchen paper. Once dry, coat them lightly in oil in a bowl with a pinch of salt and roast in the oven until golden and popping out of their shells.

giant pumpkin pasty

This cheesy pumpkin-filled pie enclosed in golden pastry looks a bit like a mammoth round Cornish pasty, hence the name. No pie tin required.

1.5 kg pumpkin (prepared weight), peeled and cut into large wedges or chunks
2 tbsp virgin rapeseed or olive oil + 1 tsp
Sea salt and freshly ground black pepper
8 cloves garlic, halved lengthways (remove the bitter sprout from the middle, if old)
4 sprigs rosemary, stripped and roughly chopped
100g Gruyère or Cheddar cheese, cut into 1cm cubes
½ tsp fennel seeds
1 organic egg, beaten, for glazing

For the pastry
270g strong white bread flour + extra for dusting
150g chilled butter, cubed
½ tsp salt
2 organic eggs
4 tbsp natural plain yoghurt

Prep tip To tackle your pumpkin, use a very sharp large knife. Cut through the stem first, then cut in half. Scoop out the seeds (see note about cooking pumpkin seeds, pagexx), then cut into large wedges. Cut the skin off of each wedge, using a downward motion with your knife. Then cut into slightly smaller chunks.

Preheat the oven to 220°C (425°F). Line a tray with baking parchment and place the pumpkin wedges on it. Drizzle with 2 tbsp oil and use your hands to coat each piece. Sprinkle with salt and pepper. Bake for 30 minutes.

Place the garlic and rosemary in a bowl and coat with 1 tsp oil. Scatter over the part-baked pumpkin. Cook for another 25–30 minutes, until the pumpkin is very soft and golden – even a few charred crusty bits will add to the flavour. Remove from the oven and leave to cool.

Meanwhile, place the flour, butter and salt in a food processor. Whizz until the mixture resembles fine crumbs. (Alternatively, work through with your fingertips.) Add the eggs and yoghurt and process briefly until a dough forms. Do not over-process. Dust a clean surface with flour and place the pastry on it. Roll into a ball, divide into two even pieces, wrap them individually in cling film and chill in the refrigerator for about 1 hour or more.

When the pumpkin is completely cool, transfer to a bowl. Mash the pumpkin with a fork, leaving it a little lumpy. Stir through the cheese cubes and fennel seed to mix evenly.

Preheat the oven to 180°C (350°F). Line a tray with baking parchment. On a lightly floured surface, roll out one piece of pastry to a 28cm circle. Place on the tray. Roll the second piece out to slightly larger than the first, about 30cm. Mound the filling on top of the bottom pastry layer, leaving a border around the edge. Place the other pastry circle on top of the filling and fold the bottom layer's edges over the top layer's edges and press to seal, twisting or crimping to make an attractive border.

Beat the egg and brush all over the pastry. Prick several times with a skewer. Bake in the centre of the oven for 45 minutes. If the glaze seems to be turning too dark during cooking, you may need to move it to a lower shelf for the duration. Serve hot or warm. **Serves 6**

NOVEMBER	INDOORS OR UNDER GLASS	OUTDOORS DIRECT IN SOI
Apples		
Broad beans		★
Broccoli (sprouting)		
Brussel sprouts		
Cabbage (winter)		
Carrots		
Cauliflower		
Celeriac		
Chard	★	
Fennel		
Fruit trees		★
Garlic		★
Kale		
Leeks		
Lettuce/salad leaves	★	
Onions/shallots		★
Oriental greens	★	
Parnsips		
Pears		
Perpetual spinach	★	
Rocket	★	
Spinach	★	
Spring onions		
Swedes		
Turnips		
Winter herbs		
Winter squashes/pumpkins		

UITABLE FOR CONTAINERS	HARVESTING NOW	RECIPES AND OTHER INFORMATION
★	★	apple + thyme tart with toffee, 150; *see also 147*
★	★	broad bean tabbouleh, 92; *see also 68, 75, 113*
★	★	psb + barley risotto, 39; *see also 35*
★	★	zesty brussels sprouts, p203; *see also 27, 42, 195*
★	★	hot + sour swede + cabbage salad, 200; *see also 191*
★	★	*see 167, 179*
★	★	cauliflower + coconut soup, 182; *see 172, 183*
★	★	celeriac gratin + ceps, 182; *see also 175*
★	★	sorrel + chard kuku, 36; *see also 32, 39, 57*
★	★	*see 140*
★		*see 181*
★		broad bean + garlic purée; *see also 39, 55, 75, 100*
★	★	saffron rice broth + winter greens, 38; *see also 42*
★	★	see 24, 45
★	★	broad beans with lettuce, 75; *see also 57, 63*
★		*see 36, 39, 75, 161*
★	★	*see 181*
★	★	parsnip, pear + stilton soup, 202; *see also 193*
★	★	chocolate upright pear cake, 184; *see also 176, 202*
★	★	*see 32*
★	★	green soup, 57; *see 46*
★	★	*see 32*
★	★	green soup, 57; *see also 61, 72, 92, 112, 131*
★	★	hot + sour swede + cabbage salad, 200; *see also 197*
★	★	*see 180*
★	★	*see 150, 169, 198*
★	★	pumpkin pasty, 169; *see also 124, 149, 162, 165, 167*

early november
ode to brassicas

Surrounding trees are starting to reveal their dark, naked limbs, and each day a blanket of crisp leaves settles over the plot. This is a welcome bonus for the compost bins and the ever-mounting leaf-mould collection. I'm still snipping a few fat pink roses from the bushes from time to time, but the hues around the lottie are fading to amber and brown.

Transcending it all, there's a swathe of aqueous blue-green foliage – the mighty brassicas are coming into their own. These hardy kings of the vegetable patch respond to the damp chill like a dose of Viagra. They pose irreverently as if to say "Winter? Bring it on!" The frost ultimately enhances their flavour, replacing bitterness with sweetness. As they begin to expand to huge proportions, they become virtually indestructible. The weeds can't compete, the birds show little interest, and their tender cores are protected from slugs by their bold outer foliage. It's true that they are hungry feeders, sucking nutrition out of the soil, and taking up a huge amount of space over a long period. But what they take from the soil, they give back on the plate with a plethora of health-enhancing nutrients including iron, fibre, vitamins, heart-disease combating antioxidants and cancer-fighting phytochemicals, not to mention their fabulous flavour. What's more, their eye-catching architecture is so welcome in the increasingly bleak lottie-scape.

It's hard to convince some people of the superlative eating qualities of the cabbage family, Brussels sprouts being a case in point. Quick cooking is the key with all brassicas, locking in the fresh mustardy flavour tones, the lively colour and an al dente texture. Overcooking intensifies the whiffy sulphur compounds released by these vegetables,

✳ cauliflower

This hungry brassica can be grown all year round, but cauliflowers are most welcome in winter months when there's not a fat lot else around. It's one disadvantage is it takes up a lot of space for a long time – nearly a year for some varieties.

I leave them to their own devices more or less, offering the usual abundance of water and some compost, and am rewarded with a few caulis. Pick them before the florets of the 'curd' start to separate. The leaves of the plant can be broken inwards and wrapped over the curd to protect it from sun (for summer varieties) or frost (for winter ones). The leaves are also edible.

Cauliflower loves a mustardy cheese sauce, especially if the cauli itself is lightly cooked. It also keeps great company with Asian flavours, especially Indian curry spices, and nuts, and takes well to being slightly charred in a wok and to oven-roasting. Soup made with onions, garlic, cauliflower, crushed cardamom seeds and coconut milk is sensational (see page 182).

Clockwise from top left Raindrops on a PSB leaf; scarlet kale; cavolo nero; scarlet kale.

'Generally, the larger the
garlic clove, the larger the
resulting bulb.'

Above and left Garlic bulbs hanging
to dry in the greenhouse.

plant garlic

Garlic is another crop that benefits from a cold spell while in the ground, so now's the time to get it in, whether it's on the plot, in the garden or in a large container outside. Seed stock, in dozens of varieties comes in the form of a bulb just like you'd use in the kitchen, which should be separated into cloves, each one producing a whole bulb. In fact I have planted garlic from the greengrocer with some good results – give it a go if you don't want to spend the money on seed stock, but it may not be a type suited to the local climate. One bulb proliferates into 12 or more bulbs – and it couldn't be easier. Just separate each clove gently and stick them in the ground individually, root end down, about 5cm deep and 10–15cm apart. Generally, the larger the garlic clove, the larger the resulting bulb. Wait about eight months and this essential ingredient will be ready to accompany all your wonderful summer and autumn veggies. You can also plant more in early spring.

make leaf mould

Once the autumn leaves have started falling on the plot or the garden, probably from about the beginning of this month, they can be raked and packed into black plastic bags until you have some that are stuffed. Perforate the bags in a few places and leave somewhere out of the way (but ideally in the light so the leaves 'cook' inside) for about a year or so to rot down – they don't look very attractive, but the result is a free and renewable source of organic matter. Leaves can also be added to the compost bin in dribs and drabs to provide fibre, which is good for soil structure.

If you haven't got access to fallen leaves, you might ask at a school or church – where someone is hired to collect leaves that are dog-mess-free – they may be able to hand them over ready-bagged.

 celeriac

Much of the edible part of celeriac grows above ground. Its tangle of spindly roots reach far beneath the surface, while it wears a tall crown of green stalky leaves, like its sisters celery, parsley and fennel. Celeriac is a bit of a troll in the vegetable world, scoring rather low in the glamour department: it's warty, hairy, wrinkly and scraggly in an endearing kind of way.

Lift with a fork, cut away the muddy roots, then the leaves, which have a strong celery taste and can be boiled in stock. Wash what's left and carve the knobbly skin off with a sharp knife.

Despite its low starch content, celeriac has a rich and creamy texture when cooked and is wonderful in soups, especially when combined with a sharp element like apple or orange. It's also good mashed with potato and butter. Grate raw celeriac and mix with mayonnaise and a dash of mustard and vinegar plus some capers and voilà, you have the French classic dish rémoulade.

mid-november
dirty weekend

We rarely get a hard frost in London, so I've never encountered a nasty shock trying to plunge a fork into frozen tundra. Any level of frost is good for breaking down the soil to a healthy texture over the winter, once dug. My soil mantra is this: feed the soil and it will feed you. It's an ongoing task to fulfil, but mid-November is ideal, with frost imminent. So Dan and I dedicate a rain-free weekend (increasingly rare now) to digging, digging, digging – breaking up and force-feeding the soil.

There is a no-dig school of organic gardening – essentially it's a matter of constantly topping up the soil with thick layers of perfectly decomposed organic matter, thus preserving the worms' complicated tunnel networks in the ground and allowing them to reign supreme as they pull in the fresh compost layers. A wonderful idea in theory, but in practice, the sheer volume of organic matter needed to adhere to this dogma is unrealistic for this urban farmer. We've got a lot of space, little time, and a degree of parsimony – it's expensive to buy enough of this stuff.

We splash out on a limited supply of good hot organic compost delivered from a local supplier and also used what we could from our own compost bins and last year's leaf mould. We scatter it evenly around the whole plot. In the empty spaces, we fork it in over a few hours, with frequent tea breaks from the thermos. At dusk, we retire home for hot toddies and a warming root vegetable potage.

✳ pears

I enjoy a few pears from the allotment each year – not from my own tree, or from a plot neighbour's, but from a branch in somebody's garden that hangs over into the site! Cheeky, I know, but they can't reach them, so why let them go to waste?

Pears are wonderful poached whole in red wine (especially Chianti) with sugar and spices, or halved and nestled in a dark-chocolate frangipane tart.

But next to munching them raw, I almost prefer them in a savoury guise, especially with cheese. One of the best salad combos I know is a bed of peppery rocket or watercress with lemon-juice-dressed pear slices, crumbled Roquefort or Stilton, a few crushed walnuts, and a sharp mustardy dressing. Their pleasantly gritty texture adds a unique quality to soups (see the recipe on page 202).

Opposite top Tools of the trade.
Opposite right My best friend the earthworm.

'My soil mantra
is this: feed the
soil and it will
feed you.'

dig and dispose

Aside from the brassica and allium beds and what's left of the root veg, there will be several vacant spaces now in the veg plot. Cold weather and in particular frost is just around the corner, and it will be great for breaking down the soil, so now's the time to dig in some nutrition. This could be well-rotted manure, leaf mould or any nutritious compost. Spread it over the surface and dig it in about one fork-length's depth. Leave the soil in clumps and the frost and worms will do the rest. Digging when the soil is wet is a no-no and will do more harm than good, especially with clay soils like mine in North London, so leave this laborious (though calorie-burning) task for dry days. Trying to dig frozen soil is a pointless exercise, obviously – though soil in the city might not freeze solid anyway. If you can't dig for whatever reason, just spreading compost over the soil for the worms to pull in over time is better than nothing.

Dead plants in containers can be removed and composted now. Some of the soil they grew in can go in the compost bin as well, depending on the size of your bin or heap; used soil shouldn't suddenly become the dominant ingredient in the bin, but it is full of useful, busy microbes. You should start with fresh potting compost next year, so out with the old, in with the new. Ideally the empty pots should then be washed, disinfected, dried and stored until next year. Makeshift recycled pots, such as plastic woven potato bags and large tins, can simply be thrown away or placed in the recycling bin. Start collecting them and begin all over again next year.

Opposite A rocket blossom in the water trough.

 carrots

Depending on the variety, it's possible to pull carrots from the soil from late May until the dead of winter. Early carrots are sweet and best eaten small and raw, while winter carrots tend to be woodier, but are still welcome on the plate or in the soup bowl. Carrots are susceptible to carrot root fly which addles them with craters, but otherwise they are a breeze to grow. Their earthy sweetness and fragrance, when freshly dug, is a revelation.

Multi-coloured heritage varieties of carrot are staging a comeback. Stumpy varieties, as pictured above, are good for clay soil.

Carrots are indeed nutritious and sweet, too. They marry well with sweet and sour fruits such as oranges, apricots and sultanas, and with spices like cinnamon, nutmeg and coriander. To me, carrot juice tastes like sweet milk. Try using carrot juice (fresh or from a carton) as a stock in which you cook seasonal vegetables and legumes with a few spices – you'll be amazed at the depth of flavour it creates.

late november
time to chill!

A gratingly cold wind is whipping through the lottie as I survey the state of it all. Fortunately there are no tasks so pressing as to threaten what's currently thriving, which is one good thing about the onset of winter. All the crops that are still going – roots, brassicas, chard and alliums – are cold-weather lovers. The weeds aren't much competition, most of the bugs have long perished, and the slugs and snails are ever-present, but not much of a match for the edible winter stalwarts. The greenhouse and coldframe are empty and dormant until spring. All is quiet, except for the odd hungry pigeon eyeing up the cabbage patch. I've got some nets and a scarecrow in place to deter them.

We attempted a fungi foray in Hampstead Heath and encountered dozens of mushrooms, but we aren't 100% certain about their edibility, so returned empty handed. We did, however, collect a brimming bag of chestnuts, which I pierced and roast in the oven. We peeled and gobbled most of them up there and then, and I saved just a few in the freezer for future concoctions.

My energies are currently focused on the hearth of the kitchen, which is logically a more amenable place to dwell in November. The harvest of the cold months is bountiful, nourishing and colourful. I've been consulting the proud culinary traditions of the northern hemisphere for recipe ideas – variations on the Ukrainian Borshch theme and hearty pies and stews using root veg, leeks, roasted onions, woody herbs and chard have entered the menu frame.

✳ turnips

Swedes and turnips are often mistaken for each other, and although they are both root crops that are technically brassicas, they are quite different vegetables requiring different treatment (see page 197). Baby turnips, roughly golf-ball size, are quite a delicacy, and are generally ready to eat earlier than swedes. Even the older ones lend a clean flavour to dishes and have a light texture, whereas swedes have a stronger, sweeter taste and a creamy texture when cooked.

You can do anything with a turnip that you would do with any other root veg, or brassica for that matter – boil, steam, sauté, fry, puree or roast. They are even lovely to eat raw, chopped finely or grated and dressed with a sharp, sweet spicy dressing of lime juice, honey and chilli or ginger, perhaps with a bit of garlic for good measure. Turnip greens, if looking fresh and healthy, can also be steamed or stir-fried.

Opposite In the UK, old faithful chard lasts through the winter.

oriental greens

Pak choi (bok choy), Chinese leaf and choi sum could all be on the menu now, if sown in August or September and protected from birds and slugs. Spicy mustard greens and tatsoi can be harvested as baby leaves for salad or cooked in stir-fries – the older the leaf, the spicier it gets.

Pak choi and Chinese leaf develop juicy stalks. Both harbour grit (unlike the supermarket specimens, which might have been hydroponically grown), so cut into long segments and wash thoroughly before stir-frying or steaming. They are best treated simply, perhaps dressed while hot with a dribble of oyster sauce from a bottle and some crisp-fried garlic or shallots.

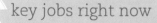

key jobs right now

plant fruit trees and bushes Now and
December is the time to get fruit planted, but don't rush into it. These plants need lots of permanent space, though once established you can leave them to their own devices more or less. Apples, pears, plums, gooseberries, and raspberry bushes can be planted now. Wait until early next year for currant bushes. Observe advice for planting disease-resistant varieties, preparing the soil appropriately and avoiding over-crowding.

cauliflower + coconut soup

A rich and memorable flavour combo – don't forget the cardamom.

Slowly fry a couple of chopped onions or leeks, add chopped garlic, then a large chopped cauliflower with salt and pepper. Sweat for about 10 minutes, then add ½ tsp cardamom seeds crushed in a mortar. Add enough liquid to cover the cauliflower, consisting of 2:1 veg stock and coconut milk. Simmer for about 20 minutes, then crush with a potato masher and serve.

celeriac gratin with ceps + chestnuts

Here's a staggeringly luxurious celeriac treatment which just screams out for the festive winter table. Or, enjoy as the focal dish, balanced with a salad a spicy rocket or steamed chard.

30g dried cep (porcini) mushrooms, rinsed
300ml boiling water
Butter for greasing gratin dish
1kg celeriac (trimmed weight), peeled and sliced as thinly as possible
Sea salt and freshly ground black pepper
100g cooked, peeled chestnuts, roughly chopped
2 tbsp chopped fresh rosemary
500ml whipping cream
75g freshly grated Parmesan

Pour the boiling water over the ceps and leave to plump for 20 minutes. Drain, reserving the liquid. Squeeze out excess water and chop the ceps roughly.

Heat the oven to 200°C (400°F). Butter a large gratin dish or casserole.

Make layers of celeriac slices in the gratin dish, sprinkling with salt, pepper, ceps, chestnuts and rosemary as you go. Finish with a layer of celeriac. Mix the reserved cep soaking liquid with the cream and pour over the celeriac. Sprinkle the Parmesan evenly over the gratin.

Bake for 50–60 minutes, or until bubbling around the edges. Test that the celeriac is fork-tender throughout before removing from the oven and leaving to stand for about 10 minutes before serving. **Serves 6–8**

Prep tip Use a sharp knife to peel the celeriac. You will invariably lose quite a bit of the vegetable in this process, as the root base harbours a lot of dirt. More than one celeriac will most likely be required to achieve the trimmed weight. The easiest way to get paper-thin slices is to use the slicing-blade fitting of a food processor. Otherwise, cut into wedges and slice by hand as thinly as you can manage.

jewelled cauliflower pilao rice

The 'jewels' in this fragrant north-Indian-inspired dish are the whole spices, sultanas, and optional sesame, coconut and pomegranate garnishes which give it a stunning finish.

250g basmati rice

2 tbsp virgin rapeseed or
  sunflower oil
1 medium onion, chopped
½ tsp cumin seed
12 whole cardamom pods
4 cloves
8–10 curry leaves, or 2 bay
  leaves
4cm piece cinnamon stick or
  a few shards of cassia bark
500g cauliflower, cut or
  broken into bite-sized
  pieces
2 tsp sea salt, or to taste

3 tbsp yellow sultanas
  (or regular)
Large pinch of saffron (about
  50 strands)
650ml water

optional garnish:
1 tbsp sesame seeds
2 tbsp unsweetened
  dessicated coconut
Handful of fresh pomegranate
  seeds

Soak the rice in cold water for 30 minutes, then drain thoroughly.

Heat a large lidded pan over a moderate flame and add oil. Cook the onion until translucent, then add the spices (not saffron). Cook until fragrant, about 1 minute, then add the cauliflower and salt and stir. Cover and let the cauliflower release some of its juices for about 5 minutes, stirring once or twice.

Now add the drained rice and sultanas and stir for 1 minute. Add the saffron and water, stir, cover and bring to the boil. The rice mixture should be just barely submerged in water; if it is not, add a little more. Bring to the boil then simmer, covered, without stirring, for 20 minutes, or until all the water is absorbed and every grain of rice is tender. Check from time to time that it has not dried out completely underneath.

To make the optional garnish, toast the sesame and coconut in a dry frying pan over a moderate flame until golden and the sesame pops. Sprinkle over the cooked pilao along with the pomegranate seeds if using.
Serves 4–6

Prep tip Cut and break up the cauliflower first, discarding the stem and core, then weigh and wash.

chocolate upright
pear cake

A rather rustic, unconventional cake with a gooey centre, this recipe uses six whole pears standing in a ring, encased in chocolate wickedness. The cake looks stunning and it should be presented whole and attacked with reckless abandon – not one for an elegant tea party. Be sure to use perfectly ripe, sweet, tender pears.

100g plain flour
1 tbsp baking powder
50g best pure cocoa powder
50g ground almonds
175g slightly salted butter, softened
175g golden caster sugar
3 organic eggs
2 tbsp milk
5 or 6 ripe pears
Cream or crème fraîche to serve (optional)

Grease a 23cm cake tin with a removable base and line the base with baking parchment. Preheat the oven to 180°C (350°F).

Sift together the flour, baking powder and cocoa over a bowl, then stir in the ground almonds.

Beat the butter and sugar together, either in a food processor or with an electric whisk, until pale and fluffy. Beat in one egg, then a spoonful of the flour mixture (to avoid curdling), then the other two eggs. Add the rest of the flour mixture and the milk and fold in or pulse until just combined, but do not over-process. Spoon into the prepared tin and spread evenly.

Cut a slice off the bottom of each pear so they will stand upright. Arrange the pears stem-side up in the batter in a ring, pushing them to the bottom of the tin, leaving about 2cm border from the edge of the tin. Place the cake on a baking sheet and cook for 45 minutes to an hour until set. The centre will remain gooey due to the pears releasing their juice – it is not undercooked. After about 15 minutes, remove from the tin and cool on a wire rack. Eat warm or cold with cream or crème fraîche, if desired.
Serves 6–8

Prep tip There's no need to core the pears as long as they are ripe – the beauty of this cake is using them core, stem, skin and all. However, once you cut the bottom off, you could use a teaspoon to scoop out the core if you must. The amount of pears used depends on their shape – arrange them in a ring of 5 or 6.

winter

WINTER	INDOORS OR UNDER GLASS	OUTDOORS DIRECT IN SO...
Broad beans		★
Broccoli (sprouting)		
Brussel sprouts		
Cabbage (winter)		
Cauliflower		
Celeriac		
Chard	★	
Fruit trees		★
Kale		
Leeks		
Lettuce/salad leaves	★	
Onions/shallots		★
Parnsips		
Perpetual spinach	★	
Rocket	★	
Salsify/scorzonera		
Spinach	★	
Spring onions		
Swedes		
Turnips		
Winter herbs		

JITABLE FOR CONTAINERS	HARVESTING NOW	RECIPES AND OTHER INFORMATION
★		broad bean tabbouleh, 92; *see also 68, 75, 113*
★	★	psb + barley risotto, 39; *see also 35*
★	★	zesty brussels sprouts, p203; *see also 27, 42, 195*
★	★	hot + sour swede + cabbage salad, 200; *see also 191*
★	★	cauliflower + coconut soup, 182; *see 172, 183*
★	★	celeriac gratin + ceps, 182; *see also 175*
★	★	sorrel + chard kuku, 36; *see also 32, 39, 57*
★		*see 181*
★	★	saffron rice broth + winter greens, 38; *see also 42*
★	★	see 24, 45
★	★	broad beans with lettuce, 75; *see also 57, 63*
★		*see 36, 39, 75, 161*
★	★	parsnip, pear + stilton soup, 202; *see also 193*
★	★	*see 32*
★	★	green soup, 57; *see 46*
★	★	*see 190*
★	★	*see 32*
★	★	green soup, 57; *see also 61, 72, 92, 112, 131*
★	★	hot + sour swede + cabbage salad, 200; *see also 197*
★	★	see 180
★	★	*see 150, 169, 198*

december
hearth-side festivities

Brrr! I've just been down to the lottie to find the water trough is a mini ice rink and every plant is glistening with frost in the morning sunbeams. I made an executive assessment of what to harvest and cook for the Christmas feast, and there is an abundance of winter veg in their prime, ready for the holiday table.

We usually spend the big day with Dan's family in Dorset, arriving on Christmas Eve with a van-load of presents (including several jars of Harvest Chutney, see page 148) and bag upon bag of allotment veg. For Christmas lunch, pheasant is usually their bird of choice, shot locally, de-feathered and gutted by my father-in-law, stuffed with a quince from a tree in their garden and roasted in the Rayburn.

For me, the real delights of the table will be the fruits of our allotment labours: cabbage and kale simmered in wine with dried fruits and spices, leeks poached in a saffron and orange sauce, Brussels sprouts cooked to perfection (see page 195), and an improvisational vegetarian celebration pie using whatever else I can muster – chard, beetroot, salsify, caramelised onions. I'll raise a glass to the bounty of our little north London allotment and to another blessed year of growing, cooking and eating.

salsify and scorzonera

These twin root vegetables, sown back in April or May, should be ready to harvest now right through to early spring. They taste much the same: salsify is pale and looks like a skinny parsnip; scorzonera has a black skin with butter-white flesh.

Rarely sale, they're worth growing if you have space. Sow as for parsnips, thin them out once the sprouts are identifiable, and then forget about them. They produce edible flowers in summer as well as young leaves. They grow deep – usually 30cm – so dig carefully.

They have a creamy texture when cooked and a vaguely sweet flavour reminiscent of Jerusalem artichoke (a crop I've yet to grow). Scrub the root and use right away, as they discolour – if not, pop into a bowl of lemony water. Cut in two or three pieces to fit in a pan of boiling, salted water, cook until tender, then rub off the skin. Cut into stubby fingers and serve simply dressed with lemon and butter.

'I'll raise a glass to the bounty of our north London allotment and to another blessed year of growing, cooking and eating.'

winter cabbages

This includes several varieties of white, red and green cabbage, including the mighty Savoy with its beautiful veiny leaves which are ideal for stuffing (see page 203). Cut winter cabbages away from the base stem and compost the outer leaves, which may be riddled with holes due to bird or slug damage. But save as many leaves as possible, as they are highly nutritious – especially dark green ones.

Winter cabbages are a little tougher than summer ones, but they can be enjoyed raw or lightly cooked if shredded. Shreds can be tossed with salt and left to drain over the sink for a while to soften before adding to salads with a light coating of vinegar and oil.

Red cabbage loves slow-cooking; it's important to include an acidic element to maintain its magenta colour. Stew with plenty of wine or vinegar and sugar, adding some fruit like apple chunks, dried apricots or sultanas or orange zest. Whole caraway, cumin, celery and dill seeds and juniper berries are all classic spices with cabbage.

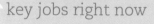

key jobs right now

cut down globe artichoke foliage

It seems brutal to decapitate these titanic plants, but conventional wisdom is that it's best to cut them right down to the ground for winter. Cover the crowns with a thick layer of leaves, straw or some kind of mulching material. Remove the mulch in late March or early April when they start to revive.

Above Hacking down the artichokes will require a hacksaw.

january
all quiet on the lottie front

In London we are at virtually the same latitude as Moscow, but the Gulf Stream affords us a milder climate – for the time being anyway, as climate change is slowing it down. Right now, daylight lasts for only eight hours or so, and very few of those are spent down on the plot, except brief visits for small harvests. Summer is such a distant memory and an even more distant expectation, but we're steadily emptying the freezer of home-grown dishes that still taste sun-drenched. I'm hibernating in my toasty warm house-cave with a full belly, snuggled up with seed catalogues and my laptop.

key jobs right now

home sprouting
Home-grown sprouts I have on the go almost all the time. They are especially welcome in winter when home-grown salad is far, far beyond the horizon. Living sprouts are full of dynamic nutrition and are easily digestible. Home sprouting is fun, quick and satisfying and infinitely cheaper than buying sprouts from a shop. The most common seeds for sprouting are alfalfa, mung bean, aduki bean, broccoli, fenugreek, radish, sunflower, mustard and cress, among others. Visit your local health food shop for seeds.

You can buy specially designed seed sprouting kits, but here's how I do it. Get yourself a very large glass jar – ask at a restaurant or cafe where they get through catering-size jars of pickles or olives – about 2 litre size is perfect. Soak the label off and wash thoroughly. Next, for a permeable lid. You know those knee-high nylon stockings? Who buys

Opposite Runner beans dried in the pod can be stored for cooking or replanted next year.

parsnips

January is the perfect time to harvest parsnips. Their flavour improves with a few frosts; beyond this time they may become woodier at the core. As soon as spring suggests itself, they start to regrow and the flavour is sucked out of the root.

I'd never heard of a parsnip until I moved to the UK from the southwest USA. I'm surprised they are not more universally loved. While other vegetables, especially those in the same family like celeriac and parsley root, may taste a little bit like parsnip, it is really a flavour unto itself. Parsnips taste like nothing else.

Scrub and peel only if you have to, cutting away any blemishes. Slice thinly and deep-fry or oven roast for crisps, then eat dipped in honey. Roasted parsnip batons or wedges are lovely with a little honey drizzled over them, or maple syrup. Or cook them in a saucepan with butter, lots of dry sherry and a little brown sugar, until the sauce reduces to a glaze. Of course they also make a fantastic soup (see page 202).

'Right now, daylight lasts for only eight hours or so, and very few of those are spent down on the plot, except brief visits for small harvests.'

those? I do! Use one knee-high as the cover for your jar. Stretch the top of the stocking over the mouth of the jar, twist the stocking and tie in a knot so that it's taut, then cut off the excess. If it seems loose around the jar's mouth, you may need to secure it with an elastic band. That's your kit.

Now for the seeds: remember they will expand to eight times their original volume or more. Rinse about 3 tablespoons of seed in cold water, then soak overnight in a bowl of water. Strain and place in the jar, then cover with the stocking, prepared as above. Lay the jar on its side, slightly propped up at the base end of the jar to let excess water run off, and cover it with a towel to exclude the light. Leave overnight again, then run cold water through the stocking to partially fill the jar, rinsing the seeds,

brussels sprouts

A high percentage of people would cite the poor Brussels sprout as their least favourite vegetable. I can understand why – they go past a point of no return if cooked too long.

I grow just one or maybe two plants a year. Like other brassicas, Brussels occupy a lot of space and are slow-growing, but well worth it, both for the sprouts and tops. In my experience, some sprouts form before others (unlike the perfect equally formed sprout-studded stalks admired at farmers' market); harvest these and leave the rest to develop. If sprouts have 'blown' or opened up, they can still be enjoyed as random greens, stir-fried, sautéed, braised or steamed, but never boiled to mush.

Cut the sprouts off the main stem. Discard any damaged leaves. Remove loose leaves from the sprouts, if you wish, to reveal the tight core, but outer leaves are quite edible. Making a shallow cross at the solid base of each sprout may reduce cooking time, but I rarely bother unless the sprouts are huge.

then drain carefully through the stocking and your fingers. Don't let the seeds stand in water – drain thoroughly and shake the seeds back into the jar from the top. Repeat this procedure twice daily until the seeds start to sprout, remove the towel then leave the jar on a windowsill. Keep rinsing twice daily until the sprouts are big enough to eat – between 4 and 6 days. That's it!

prune fruit trees Now is the time for a pruning job on most fruit trees and bushes, while the plants are dormant. This includes: apples, currants, gooseberries, plums, raspberries, pears and grape vines. The aim is to improve their health by removing dead growth and reducing overcrowded branches, but techniques vary from fruit to fruit, so seek advice about your specific variety.

february
winter's final chapter

It's still cold, but the nights are noticeably drawing out, rather than in. My seed potatoes have arrived and are chitting away happily. Mostly I'm keeping warm in the kitchen, cooking up the winter harvest and freezer fodder, fantasising about what's to come. I'm looking forward to shifting some of the layers both beneath my skin and on top of it as I get busy in the garden, but I'll have to wait just a few more weeks…

 swedes

key jobs right now

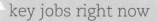

clean the greenhouse If you are itching for a job on the plot on an icy February day – or sometime before March – hose down the inside and outside of the greenhouse if you have one. Spray with disinfectant and squeegee the panels. This ensures against disease and infestation next year.

divide and plant or force rhubarb
Rhubarb is best started from an existing crown rather than from seed, and crowns can be planted until March. It is not recommended for containers but, planted in the ground, it is easy, perennial, prolific and trouble-free. The only advisable rhubarb maintenance, though not essential, is to divide existing crowns which are five years old or more to make them more vigorous, which simply multiplies the plant. This is done by lifting the crown out of the soil and slicing it into three pieces with two swift vertical strokes of a spade. Re-plant the crowns in their new permanent positions just below the surface. Give them plenty of TLC in the form of well-rotted compost and water.

Clockwise from top left Cucumber plants; thyme; brassicas such as scarlet kale will begin to flower as soon as there's a hit of spring in the air; scarlet kale blossom.

This veg confuses. Some equate it to turnip (see page 180), but it's different. The Scots are one of few cultures to appreciate its merits; it is the core ingredient in bashed neeps, served on Burn's Night with haggis. 'Neeps' should be 'pars-neeps', surely? No. Swedes, which the Scots sometimes call tur-neeps.

The swede (aka rutabaga) is often considered a root vegetable, when in fact it's a brassica and should be treated as such when considering crop rotation.

To clarify, swede is larger and more rotund than its turnip cousin, with a purple blush and apricot flesh. It is sweeter, richer and creamier in texture than turnip. Most banish it to the 'only fit for cattle fodder' category, but I say, "Give swede a chance!"

Strictly a winter veg, home-grown swedes never reach the proportions of those commercially grown, but bring satisfaction in having something to dig up midwinter.

It makes a lovely mash if enriched with butter and milk, or better still, cream.

If you have more than one established crown, you can force one (not recently planted ones) as soon as you see some new growth appear later this month or in February. Cover the crown with a large upturned vessel like a giant pot or dustbin to exclude the light, and the plant will desperately throw out very sweet bright pink stalks in a few weeks – the first crop of the new year, which is quite exciting. Harvest these by pulling them from the crown over a couple of weeks, then remove the covering and let the plant carry on as normal. The disadvantage is, if you have forced it, you really shouldn't pull much more from it – let it recharge and don't force the same plant again year after year. This is why you should only force it if you have more than one plant, because you don't want to miss out on all the 'rhubarb-liciousness' coming up over the spring months!

winter herbs

Woody, evergreen herbs such as rosemary, thyme, bay and sage are available year-round, but are so welcome in winter to invigorate soups and roasted dishes. To me these are 'oily herbs' because they contain pungent, waxy oils which sustain them through all weather conditions.

Rosemary works beautifully with winter vegetables and breads, but needn't be restricted to savoury dishes. A chopped handful added to biscuits and cakes is a revelation. Thyme, too, applies itself gloriously to autumn fruits (see the recipe on page 150).

Bay is best infused into stocks and sauces to add another dimension – when making a bechamel, simmer milk with fresh bay leaves first.

Sage makes a winter pesto with walnuts instead of the traditional pinenuts and basil (add a touch of lemon juice to balance the flavour).

When making a soup or stew, grab a sprig of each of these herbs, tie together with string and simmer in the liquid for a whole new dimension.

order seeds for your new gardening year

This can be done any time over the winter months. You don't need to get everything now, just the seeds you want to get started in early spring, including potatoes, lettuces, brassicas and sun-loving plants like tomatoes (see spring sowing charts at the beginning of each chapter). I find ordering from catalogues online is better than buying from a garden centre, because you get more in-depth descriptions – how they grow, when they crop, how they taste etc, and you can compare them side-by-side. Sometimes you can get good deals on groups of seed packets as well, plus free bonus packets.

Consider it carefully. First, examine what seeds you have left over from last year and check use-by dates – and heed them. Ask yourself, what have I realistically got space for? What thrives in my space and my soil? What will I be growing in containers? What were the most delicious crops from last year and do I want those again? Do I have time to be adventurous with some oddball crops and if so, can I realistically grow them in my conditions?

When choosing tomatoes, be careful whether you are choosing cordon (indeterminate) or bush (determinate) varieties. Cordon types need strong support and constant pruning for a good crop, which is more time- and space-consuming.

Once you've filled your virtual shopping trolley, check the total price – you may be rather alarmed and decide to pare it down a bit. You can always order more later – for once it's better to have not enough than too many that just go to waste.

Finally, let yourself get excited! Whether you're starting from scratch, embarking on your second year, or feeding a well-oiled machine of experience, each year is a completely different journey on the urban farm, and you can take your very own expedition into the wild world of growing your own. Good luck!

'Each year is a completely different journey on the urban farm, and you can take your very own expedition into the wild world of growing your own.'

Above Open seed packets should only be reused next year providing they're within their use-by date. Store in a cool dry place.

hot + sour swede + cabbage salad

A colourful, crunchy, high-impact salad to brighten a winter's day. Raw grated swede adds a surprisingly good flavour to this Asian-style salad. Coriander is the ideal herb for this salad but parsley is more likely to be growing in winter.

2 tbsp sesame seeds

200g red cabbage, finely shredded

200g swede, peeled and coarsely grated
2 spring onions, finely sliced
3–4 mild red chillies, chopped
Handful of parsley or coriander, finely chopped

For the dressing
3 tbsp shoyu or light soy sauce
2 tbsp rice vinegar
2 tbsp unrefined caster sugar
1 tbsp sesame oil

50g toasted peanuts, to finish

Toast the sesame seeds. Place them in a small frying pan over a medium heat, stirring and shaking the pan until golden and popping. Remove to a plate to cool.

Combine the cabbage, swede, onions, chillies, parsley and sesame seeds. Beat together the dressing ingredients and stir through the salad. Pound the peanuts in a mortar until crushed. Divide the salad amongst four plates and sprinkle with peanuts. **Serves 4**

Prep tip Remove any ropey outer leaves from the cabbage. Cut the cabbage in half first, then cut out the solid core and discard to the compost container. Place one half cut side down, cut in half once more top to bottom, slice finely cutting downward, then weigh the 200g.

parsnip, pear + stilton soup

These three kings of the winter table somehow add up to more than the sum of their parts in this luxuriously rich soup – definitely a meal in itself served with some rustic, crusty bread.

50g butter
2 large onions, chopped
1 tbsp fresh thyme leaves
3 celery sticks, chopped
1kg parsnips, scrubbed and
    chopped
2 pears, cored, chopped and
    dressed with the juice of
    ½ a lemon
Sea salt and freshly ground
    pepper
1.5 litres vegetable stock
200g Stilton, coarsely
    crumbled

Heat a large pan over a low to medium heat and melt the butter. Add the onions with the thyme and gently soften until translucent. Add the celery, parsnips and some salt and pepper, cover and sweat for 10 minutes, stirring occasionally. Add the pears with the lemon juice and the stock. Bring to the boil and simmer for half an hour. Cool briefly, then puree until completely smooth. Ladle into warm bowls and sprinkle the crumbled Stilton on top of each. **Serves 6**

Prep tip If possible, for the best flavour, leave the skin on the parsnips. Just scrub thoroughly and cut out any blemishes. The skin can be left on the pears as well.

lemony lentil cabbage parcels

Sweet caramelised onions offset the soft lemony red lentil filling, encapsulated in striking Savoy cabbage leaves. Serve as part of a mezze platter, or with rice, a rich tomato sauce and thick yoghurt.

200g red lentils, rinsed
1 Savoy cabbage
3 large onions (600g approx), halved and sliced
1 tbsp olive oil + more for greasing baking dish
2 tsp sugar
Finely grated zest and juice of one large lemon
Sea salt and freshly ground black pepper
50g butter, melted

Put a large pan of water on to boil and salt it well.

Place the lentils in a small lidded saucepan and just cover with water. Bring to the boil and skim off the foam. Boil rapidly for 10 minutes, stirring from time to time, then reduce to a simmer, add some salt and cover. Add a bit more water if they seem to be drying out. Simmer for about 15 minutes, stirring occasionally. The resulting consistency should be like thick porridge. Remove from the heat.

Meanwhile, cut 12 cabbage leaves carefully away from the core at the base of the leaf, discarding any tough outer leaves. Shave down any particularly thick stems with a paring knife. Wash the leaves, then blanch them, a few at a time, in the boiling water for 2 minutes only, using tongs to handle them. Refresh the leaves under a stream of cold water and drain in a colander.

Heat a frying pan over a medium heat and add the olive oil. Add the onions and fry, stirring frequently. When they start to go brown, add the sugar. Stir them attentively until nicely caramelised. In a bowl, combine the caramelised onions, cooked lentils, lemon juice and zest. Taste and season.

Preheat the oven to 180°C (350°F) and brush a baking dish with oil. Pat dry each cabbage leaf. Place a heaped spoonful of filling in the middle near the base of the leaf. Fold over the sides, then roll up. Place seam-side down in the baking dish. Brush lightly with melted butter. Bake for 20–25 minutes until lightly browned. Serve hot, warm, or at room temperature. **Serves 4–6**

zesty brussels sprouts

Voilà! The much-maligned Brussels sprouts become ambrosia.

Put the prepared sprouts in a lidded pan with very little water, add a generous knob of butter, some salt, a couple of spoonfuls of sugar and quite a lot of freshly grated lemon zest. Don't start to cook until very close to serving time. This is usually the death of them, if they are cooked too early and left to turn to mush. When you are ready, put the covered pan over a high flame, bring to the boil, reduce to a simmer, stirring gently once or twice, until just bright green and tender – 3–5 minutes depending on quantity – and serve ASAP.

Recommended Suppliers

Chase Organics http://www.chaseorganics.co.uk
Chiltern Seeds http://www.chilternseeds.co.uk
Garden Centre Online
   http://www.gardencentreonline.co.uk
Harrod Horticultural http://www.harrodhorticultural.com
Moles Seeds http://www.molesseeds.co.uk
Sarah Raven's Kitchen and Garden
   http://www.sarahraven.com
Sea Spring Seeds http://www.seaspringseeds.co.uk
Seeds of Italy http://www.seedsofitaly.com
The Organic Gardening Catalogue
   www.organiccatalog.com
The Real Seed Catalogue http://www.realseeds.co.uk
Two Wests & Elliot http://www.twowests.co.uk

Further Reading

Growing Stuff: An Alternative Guide to Gardening, Black Dog 2009
Air, Donna (ed.), *Grown In Britain Cookbook*, Dorling Kindersley 2008
Berger, Susan, *Allotment Gardening*, Green Books 2005
Bridgewater, A. & G., *The Allotment Specialist*, New Holland 2007
Caplin, Adam and Brooks Brown, Celia, *New Kitchen Garden*,
   Ryland, Peters & Small 2003
Clevely, Andi, *The Allotment Book*, HarperCollins 2006
Davidson, Max Adam, *The Gardener*,
   Beaverbrook Newspapers Ltd. 1976
Dirty Nails, *How to Grow Your Own Food*, Spring Hill 2007
Dowding, Charles, *Organic Gardening The Natural No-Dig Way*,
   Green Books 2007
Fowler, Alys, *The Thrifty Gardener*, Kyle Cathie 2008
Harland, Gail and Larrinua-Craxton, Sofia, *The Tomato Book*,
   Dorling Kindersley 2009
Harrison, John, *Vegetable Growing Month by Month*, Right Way
   2008
Hemphill, Rosemary, *Herbs for All Seasons*, Penguin 1975
Hessayon, Dr. D.G., *The Vegetable and Herb Expert*,
   Expert Books 1997
Hessayon, Dr. D.G., *The Fruit Expert*, Expert Books 1993
Merrett, Paul, *Using the Plot*, HarperCollins 2008
Michael, Pamela, *Edible Wild Plants & Herbs*, Grub Street 2007
Ott, Steve, Rawlings, Emma and Warwick, Roxanne, *Grow Your
   Own Fruit & Veg in Plot, Pot or Growbags*, Foulsham 2008
Popescu, Charlotte, *Vegetables: Grow Them, Cook Them, Eat
   Them*, Cavalier Paperbacks 2004
Raven, Sarah, *Sarah Raven's Garden Cookbook*, Bloomsbury 2007
Warren, Piers, *How to Store Your Garden Produce*,
   Green Books 2003
Watson, Guy and Baxter, Jane, *Riverford Farm Cook Book*,
   Fourth Estate 2008

Editorial Director Jane O'Shea
Creative Director Helen Lewis
Project Editor Lisa Pendreigh
Designer Claire Peters
Design Assistant Katherine Case
Photographer Jill Mead
Food stylist Celia Brooks Brown
Stylist Charis White
Production Director Vincent Smith
Production Controller Ruth Deary

First published in 2010 by
Quadrille Publishing Limited
Alhambra House
27–31 Charing Cross Road
London WC2H 0LS
www.quadrille.co.uk

Text © 2010 Celia Brooks Brown
Photography © 2010 Jill Mead
Design and layout © 2010 Quadrille
Publishing Ltd

Cataloguing in Publication Data: a catalogue
record for this book is available from the
British Library.

ISBN 978 184400 817 9

Printed in China

My heart is brimming with thanks to all who sowed the seeds for this book and helped it grow and blossom.

Firstly, thanks to Nick Wyke at Timesonline for allowing me to create my New Urban Farmer persona, and for your ongoing encouragement and discipline.

Thanks to my agent Martine Carter for introducing me to the wonderful people at Quadrille Publishing.

Heartfelt thanks to the Quadrille team: Jane O'Shea, for turning a vision into reality; Claire Peters, for your effortless talent and keen eye; Lisa Pendreigh, for your patience, good humour and astute editorial support; and Charis White for the fantastic props. Thank you Quadrille for finding the brilliant photographer Jill Mead – an inspired pairing. Jill, thanks for capturing the spirit of this book so beautifully. What fun we had!

Thanks to all of my lottie neighbours – I'm so fortunate to be flanked by such a lovely bunch: Ulrika, Fred, Miss Gaynor, Alex, Lloyd, Suzanne, and Soraya. Thanks to John and Rena for looking out for the plot and for friendship.

And of course thank you Dan, my love, my rock.

Thanks to Eric Treuille and the Books for Cooks team for the inspiration behind Chocolate Upright Pear Cake; to Erin McGann for installing the original idea behind Warm Courgette Salad with Parmesan Crackling; to Lizzie Mabbot for pointing me to your dad's rhubarb mince dish; and to Jeanne Brown, mistress of preserving and model glut-buster.

Mom, thanks for your devoted analysis and just for letting me be me!

Finally, thanks to all the incredible people who tested recipes so diligently and gave me such constructive feedback. I'm bowled over by your enthusiasm and kindness: Ali and Paul Middleton, Callum Saunders, Cara Waters, Claire Sutton, Danny Kingston, Derek Thomas, Elizabeth Coulter, Elizabeth Shepard, Gail Francis, Helen 'a forkful of spaghetti', Helen Graves, Helen Yuet Ling Pang, Ian Fischer, Jennifer Farnell, Linda Williams, Lizzie Mabbot, Michelle Eshkeri of Lavender Bakery, Niamh Shields, Nora Ryan, Patrick Barber, Rejina Juie Sabur, Roslyn Henry, Shaheen Safdar, Stephanie Pennington, and Tami Duquette.